Four Essays on
Gulliver's Travels

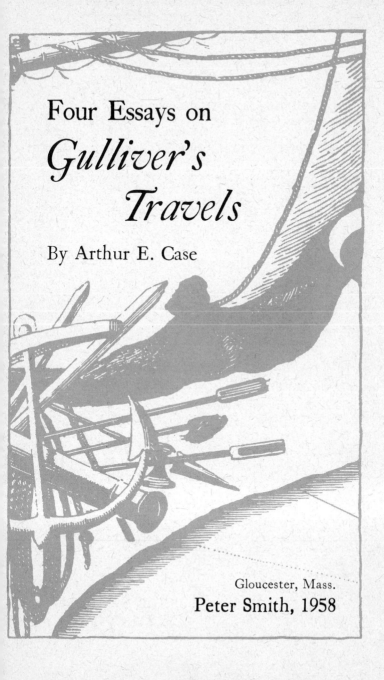

Four Essays on
*Gulliver's
Travels*

By Arthur E. Case

Gloucester, Mass.
Peter Smith, 1958

To

Frederick Benjamin Kaye

1 8 9 2 - 1 9 3 0

and

Warren Hiram Lowenhaupt

Preface

These essays are the consequence of an edition of *Gulliver's Travels* which I undertook some years ago with no expectation of reaching any important new conclusions about the book. In the course of preparing the edition, however, I found myself in disagreement with modern criticism at a number of points. Most of my beliefs about these matters were incorporated in my edition, but in such brief form that it seems worth while to publish this more extended argument in support of my contentions. I have added a few minor ideas to those which I announced some seven years ago, and in one or two instances I have slightly modified what I then said, but these are changes of detail only: some of them have already been incorporated in later printings of my edition.

I acknowledge with gratitude and pleasure the grant which Northwestern University has provided to assist in the publication of these essays.

Contents

The Text of Gulliver's Travels

ON a night in the late summer or early fall of the year 1726 Mr. Benjamin Motte, master printer of London, came into the possession of an important manuscript under unusual circumstances, which Alexander Pope recounted to his friend Jonathan Swift in a letter written on November 16.[1] "Motte received the copy," wrote Pope, "he tells me, he knew not from whence, nor from whom, dropped at his house in the dark, from a hackney coach." The "copy" was the manuscript of a book with a long title, since shortened by the world to two words—*Gulliver's Travels*.

The mysterious appearance of the manuscript was, in point of fact, no more a mystery to Motte than it was to Swift. It was merely the culmination of a series of moves by Swift and his friends intended to guard the author from political persecution of the sort which had recently threatened him in connection with the *Drapier's Letters*. As far back as September 29, 1725, Swift had written to Pope, "I have employed my time, besides ditching, in finishing, correcting, amending, and transcribing my Travels, in four parts complete, newly augmented, and intended for the press, when the world shall deserve them, or rather when a printer shall be found brave enough to venture his ears."[2] In the same letter he dropped a hint that he might soon visit England. But illness intervened, and Swift obviously did not care to trust his book to any other hands than his own. So it was not until March, 1726, that Swift set foot on the soil of England for the first time in more than eleven years.[3] Shortly after his landing he was in London, greeting his close friends of the last years of the Queen—Arbuthnot, Gay, and Pope. Arbuthnot first took him

in charge for a round of visits to the politicians—to Lord
Chesterfield, to William Pulteney, to Viscount Bolingbroke,
now returned from his long exile in France and settled at his
new country-seat at Dawley. Then in May it was Pope's turn,
and until Swift went back to Ireland in the middle of August
he made Twickenham his headquarters, going on occasional
"rambles" in the company of Pope and Gay to the country
houses of friends, or making short excursions to London on
business. What happened to the manuscript of *Gulliver* during
these months is a matter for conjecture. It is not very bold to
assume that Swift's most intimate friends, Pope and Gay,
read the book and offered suggestions. Charles Ford, the
Irishman in whom Swift had confided most freely during
the writing of the *Travels*, was in England at the time, and
may well have had a part in the consultations of the summer.[4]
All three men were involved in the negotiations with Motte,
as will appear later. Arbuthnot and Bolingbroke might have
been expected to take a hand in any revisions of the book
before its publication, but there are indications that neither
of them did, though both of them knew the general design
and many of the details.[5]

Minor alterations in and additions to the manuscript of the
Travels may have taken up some of Swift's time at Twickenham, but the fact that Motte was not approached until August
suggests that other things were afoot. It is, of course, possible
that some other publisher was sounded out first: this, however, is unlikely, as Motte was the successor in business of
Swift's old friend and publisher, Benjamin Tooke, and was
therefore the natural person for Swift to turn to.[6] More
probably a good deal of the time was occupied, as Professor
Quintana has suggested, in the copying of the manuscript by
an amanuensis, in order that Swift's handwriting might not
be recognized by the authorities in case of a prosecution.[7]
Swift often employed this device, and had recently been using
it in connection with the *Drapier's Letters*.[8] The manuscript
of *Gulliver* was unusually long, however, and Swift may have
preferred to send his own fair copy to the printer, trusting to
him to get rid of it before the book was issued.

Whatever the reason for the delay, the negotiations with Motte began during the second week of August. The correspondence, so far as it has been preserved, follows:

Sir,   *London, August 8, 1726*

My cousin, Mr. Lemuel Gulliver, entrusted me some years ago with a copy of his travels, whereof that which I here send you is about a fourth part, for I shortened them very much, as you will find in my Preface to the Reader. I have shown them to several persons of great judgement and distinction, who are confident they will sell very well; and, although some parts of this and the following volumes may be thought in one or two places to be a little satirical, yet it is agreed they will give no offence; but in that you must judge for yourself, and take the advice of your friends, and if they or you be of another opinion, you may let me know it when you return these papers, which I expect shall be in three days at furthest. The good report I have received of you makes me put so great a trust into your hands, which I hope you will give me no reason to repent, and in that confidence I require that you will never suffer these papers to be once out of your sight.

As the printing these Travels will probably be of great value to you, so, as a manager for my friend and cousin, I expect you will give a due consideration for it, because I know the author intends the profit for the use of poor seamen, and I am advised to say that two hundred pounds is the least sum I will receive on his account; but if it shall happen that the sale will not answer, as I expect and believe, then whatever shall be thought too much, even upon your own word, shall be duly repaid.

Perhaps you may think this a strange way of proceeding to a man of trade, but since I begin with so great a trust to you, whom I never saw, I think it not hard that you should trust me as much; therefore, if after three days' reading and consulting these papers you think it proper to stand to my agreement, you may begin to print them, and the subsequent parts shall be all sent you one after another in less than a week, provided that immediately upon your resolution to print them you do within three days deliver a bank-bill of two hundred pounds, wrapped up so as to make a parcel, to the hand from whence you receive this, who will come in the same manner exactly at nine o'clock at night on Thursday, which will be the 11th instant.

If you do not approve of this proposal, deliver these papers to the person who will come on Thursday. If you choose rather to send the papers, make no other proposal of your own, but just barely write on a piece of paper that you do not accept my offer. I am, Sir,

Your humble servant,

FOR MR. MOTTE[9]   RICHARD SYMPSON

[August 11, 1726]

I return you, Sir, your papers with a great many thanks, and do assure you that since they have been in my custody I have faithfully deserved the good opinion you expressed of my integrity; but you were much mistaken in the estimate you made of my abilities when you supposed me able in vacation time, the most dead season of the year, at so short notice to deposit so considerable a sum as two hundred pounds. By delivering the papers to the bearer I have put you in entirely the same condition they [*sic*] were in before I saw them, but if you will trust my promise or accept any security you can contrive or require for the payment of the money in six months, I will comply with any method you shall propose for that purpose. In the mean time I shall trust to your honour and promise that what shall appear to be more than the success of it deserves shall be repaid, as you may depend upon a proper acknowledgment if the success answers or exceeds expectation. I have only to add that before I received your letter I had fixed a journey into the country, and wrote to some dealers there to appoint times when I should call upon them, so that I shall be obliged to set out this day sennight at furthest; therefore if you think fit to favour me with any further correspondence desire I may hear from you as soon as possible, that the book shall be published within a month after I receive the copy, and if the success will allow it, I will punctually pay the money you require in six months. I shall thankfully embrace the offer. The bearer stays for an answer so that I can only offer a proposal without giving a reason. I am, Sir,

Your humble servant.

B. MOTTE[10]

August 13, 1726

I would have both volumes come out together, and published by Christmas at farthest.

TO MR. MOTTE[11]   R. SYMPSON

This fragmentary and inconclusive correspondence leaves uncertain the date on which matters were finally settled. No doubt "Richard Sympson" was the signature which represented Swift and his Twickenham friends, though tradition has it that the actual messenger was either Erasmus Lewis or Charles Ford.[12] Swift returned to Ireland in August[13] while certain details were still undecided, leaving the conclusion of the arrangements in the hands of Pope. As late as September 16 Gay wrote to Swift, "As for the particular affair that you want to be informed in, we are as yet wholly in the dark; but Mr. Pope will follow your instructions."[14] And in May, 1735, Swift informed Pulteney, "I never got a farthing by anything I writ, except one about eight years ago, and that was by Mr. Pope's prudent management for me."[15] Probably the final bargain was struck shortly after Gay's letter: if so, Motte fulfilled his promise to publish the book within a month by issuing it on October 28, 1726.[16]

The circumstances surrounding the publication of *Gulliver* made it impracticable for either Swift or his friends to correct the press. The best evidence that no friend did so is the fact that Motte deliberately made a number of important changes in the text. Most of the alterations were intended to lessen the chance of prosecution, and for this reason they are interesting as showing what the printer believed to be politically dangerous. The chief passages involved were the description of the colored "silken Threads" which distinguished the various orders in Lilliput (1.3.4),[17] the account of the cryptographers of Tribnia (3.6.12), a gibe at Parliament (3.7.9), the sneer at German mercenary troops (4.5.5), the long attack on law and lawyers (4.5.10-17) and the remarks about Queen Anne and prime ministers (4.6.10-13): the allegory of the fight over Wood's halfpence (3.3.14-18) was omitted altogether. For some reason now unknown Swift attributed the changes to the pen of the Reverend Mr. Andrew Tooke, a schoolmaster and a son of Benjamin Tooke.[18]

Aside from intentional alterations the printing of the first edition seems to have been more than ordinarily careful and conscientious. Some literal errors were corrected while the book was passing through the press: one of the two canceled leaves in the second volume (E8 in the fourth voyage) was reprinted for no other reason than that it contained one error in sense and one stylistic infelicity.[19] Nevertheless Swift was dissatisfied. Undoubtedly at his request and perhaps at his dictation, Ford wrote to Motte from Dublin on January 3, 1726-7:

Sir,

I bought here Captain Gulliver's Travels published by you, both because I heard much talk of it, and because of a rumour that a friend of mine is suspected to be the author. I have read this book twice over with great care, as well as great pleasure, and am sorry to tell you it abounds with many gross errors of the press, whereof I have sent you as many as I could find, with the corrections of them as the plain sense must lead, and I hope you will insert them if you make another edition.

I have an entire respect for the memory of the late Queen, and am always pleased when others show the same; but that paragraph relating to her looks so very much beside the purpose that I cannot think it to have been written by the same author. I wish you and your friends would consider it, and let it be left out in the next edition; for it is plainly false in fact, since all the world knows that the Queen during her whole reign governed by one first Minister or other. Neither do I find the author to be anywhere given to flattery, or indeed very favourable to any Prince or Minister whatsoever.

These things I let you know out of perfect good will to the author and yourself, and I hope you will so understand me, who am, Sir,

Your affectionate friend and servant,

CHA. FORD.

TO MR. BENJAMIN MOTTE, BOOKSELLER,
NEAR THE TEMPLE IN LONDON.[20]

The list Ford speaks of in his letter (which, together with the letter itself, is now in the Victoria and Albert Museum) supplies minor corrections in full, but merely refers to longer incorrect passages, as if Ford assumed that Motte still had the manuscript and could make the necessary alterations by comparing the printed with the written text.[21] This is of some

importance, because the list is very often identified with
Ford's "paper,"[22] which Ford describes in a letter to Swift on
November 6, 1733: "I lent Mr. Corbett that paper to correct
his Gulliver by, and it was from it that I mended my own.
There is every single alteration from the original copy. . . ."
As Ford's annotated copy (also in the Victoria and Albert
Museum) has the corrections of even the longer passages in
full it is clear that his "paper," now unfortunately lost, was
closer to the original manuscript than either the "list" he sent
to Motte or his own annotated copy of the first edition. This
copy has the shorter corrections written into the margins. The
longer corrections are written on blank pages bound into the
book, not always near the printed passage to which they refer,
so that there are, in Ford's words, "perpetual references
backwards and forwards."[23] As might be expected, there are
some small variations between the "list" and the annotated
copy.

In the next edition after the receipt of Ford's letter Motte
adopted practically all the corrections which were fully set
out in the "list," and made this the occasion for advertising
"the second edition corrected." (It was, as a matter of fact,
the fourth.)[24] But in those cases in which Ford had merely
indicated that a passage was incorrect without supplying the
correct text Motte retained the reading of the first edition,
even when the reading of the manuscript could hardly have
been regarded as dangerous. It may be that Motte did not
wish to take the trouble of looking through the manuscript
for the original text, but this seems unlikely in view of his
care with other parts of the revised edition. More probably his
copy of the manuscript had already disappeared, either
through carelessness of the printers, notorious in those times,
or because the manuscript was in Swift's holograph and
Motte had felt it prudent to destroy it.[25]

Motte made an excellent thing of *Gulliver*. Gay and Pope
reported to Swift that the first edition was sold off in a
week,[26] and the second and third (both, like the first, octavos
dated 1726) followed so swiftly that neither had the benefit
of Ford's corrections, which presumably reached London

about the middle of January, 1727. At this time Motte seems already to have printed a duodecimo edition for the cheaper trade, but he withheld this until he had issued the revised octavo of 1727. The second octavo had been set up from the first, and the third from the second: the duodecimo was probably, though not certainly, set from a copy of the third octavo. The revised octavo, however, was set from a copy of the first edition which had the original leaf D8 in the second volume: as already noted, it had the benefit of the minor corrections in the list sent by Ford. This was the last edition of *Gulliver* manufactured by Motte, though he issued the duodecimo in 1727, and reissued it in 1731 with new title pages. Probably his market, after 1727, was somewhat damaged by the various pirated editions, including at least two in serial form, which appeared in London and Dublin.[27]

During these years the relations between Swift and Motte became increasingly cordial. Six months after the publication of the *Travels* Motte made, through Erasmus Lewis, a satisfactory financial settlement. On July 15, 1732, Swift wrote to the publisher:

> Upon my word, I never intended that any but yourself should be concerned as printer or bookseller in anything that shall be published with my consent while I am alive, or after my death by my executors. As to my posthumous things I shall intrust them to Mr. Pope, but with a strong recommendation that you alone may be employed, supposing and being assured of your honest and fair dealing, which I have always found. I am likewise desirous that some time or other all that I acknowledge to be mine in prose and verse, which I shall approve of, with any little things that shall be thought deserving, should be published by themselves by you during my life, if it contains any reasonable time, provided you are sure it will turn to your advantage; and this you may say to Mr. Pope, as my resolution, unless he hath any material objections to it, which I would desire to know. For I ever intended the property as a bookseller should be only in you, as long as you shall act with justice and reason, which I have never doubted in the least, and I conceive that Mr. Pope's opinion of you is the same with mine.[28]

By December 9 of this year, however, when Swift wrote again to Motte, a new factor had entered into the calculations.

> I believe I told you formerly that booksellers here [in Dublin] have no property, and I have cause to believe that some of our printers will collect all they think to be mine, and print them by subscription, which I will neither encourage nor oppose. But as to the writings I have had long by me, I intend to leave them to certain friends, and that you shall be the publisher.[29]

The chief Dublin printer to whom Swift referred was George Faulkner. The manner of his proposal to print the Dean's works is described in a letter from Swift to Pope:

> The Collection you speak of is this. A printer came to me to desire he might print my works, as he called them, in four volumes by subscription. I said I would give no leave, and should be sorry to see them printed here. He said they could not be printed in London. I answered they could, if the partners agreed. He said, he would be glad of my permission, but as he could print them without it, and was advised that it could do me no harm, and having been assured of numerous subscriptions, he hoped I would not be angry at his pursuing his own interest, etc. Much of this discourse passed, and he goes on with the matter, wherein I determined not to intermeddle, though it be much to my discontent, and I wish it could be done in England, rather than here, although I am grown pretty indifferent in everything of that kind. This is the truth of the story.[30]

On February 16, 1732-3, Swift gave Faulkner a letter to the Earl of Oxford which indicated that the project was under way:

> The bearer, Mr. Faulkner, the prince of Dublin printers, will have the honour to deliver you this. He tells me your Lordship was so gracious as to admit him into your presence, and receive him with great condescension, which encouraged him to hope for the same favour again by my mediation, which I could not refuse. Although for his own profit he is engaged in a work that very much discontents me, yet I would rather have it fall into his hands, than any other's on this side.[31]

These last two letters afford good examples of Swift's mixed attitude toward Faulkner's project from first to last. Despite his protestations of indifference, it is clear that he wished to see a collected edition of his works, provided he could control its contents. It is equally clear that he would have preferred to have that edition published in London, not only because he liked and trusted Motte and knew that he would do a better job of printing than could be done in Dublin, but also because he cared more about the opinion of the English reading public than he did about any other. No doubt he also disliked the realization that he could not stop Faulkner if the latter chose to proceed. The printer's argument, it must be admitted, had in it a little of Peachum's when he tried to induce Polly to betray Macheath: "Since the thing sooner or later must happen, I dare say the captain himself would like that we should get the reward for his death sooner than a stranger."

On the other hand, Faulkner's approach had been perfectly frank and reasonable. He had had previous dealings with Swift, who seems to have liked him and to have had a good opinion of his honesty. If he was determined to go ahead, as he apparently was, there were obvious advantages in having him continue his deferential attitude, and in putting him under such obligations that it would be more profitable for him to follow Swift's instructions than to disobey them. There would be a chance, too, of restoring the passages in *Gulliver* which Motte, more accessible to the avenging powers of the English government, had omitted or "softened" through fear; and a general supervision of the whole edition would be far easier if the printing were done close at hand. Swift's Irish patriotism was also involved, as will be seen when Motte and Faulkner come into direct conflict in 1735. And lastly, there was the undeniable fact that the various English owners of "property" in Swift's writings showed no sign of coming to an agreement over a complete edition. Swift was sixty-five, and he fancied that his faculties were decaying. If he were to oversee a collection of his works it would have to be soon.

And so, grudgingly and intermittently, he began to co-operate with Faulkner. A letter of June 29, 1733, shows him directing the printer (mistakenly, as it turned out) to the Pilkingtons for an interleaved copy of the *Travels*.[32] Three months later he begins a correspondence with Ford on the same subject:

Swift to Ford, October 9, 1733.

. . . If I had been well I should have writ to you a good while ago, upon an occasion that perhaps you may have heard of in Advertisements. A Printer of this Town applyed himself to me by letters and friends for leave to print in four volumes the works of J S D D, &c. I answered that as I could not hinder him, so I would not encourage him, but that he should take care not to charge me with what I never writ. There is no Propriety of Copyes here; they print what they please. The man behaved himself with all respect, and since it was an evil I could not avoyd, I had rather they should be printed correctly than otherwise. Now, you may please to remember how much I complained of Motts suffering some friend of his (I suppose it was Mr Took a Clergy-man now dead) not onely to blot out some things that he thought might give offence, but to insert a good deal of trash contrary to the Author's manner and Style, and Intention. I think you had a Gulliver interleaved and set right in those mangled and murdered Pages. I inquired afterwards of severall Person[s] where that Copy was; some said Mr Pilkington had it, but his Wife sent me word she could not find it. Other[s] said it was in Mr Corbet's hands. On my writing to him, he sent a loose Paper with very little except literall corrections in your hand. I wish you would please to let me know, whether You have such an interleaved Gulliver; and where and how I could get [it] ; For to say the truth, I cannot with patience endure that mingld and mangled manner, as it came from Mottes hands; and it will be extreme difficult for me to correct it by any other means, with so ill a memory, and in so bad a State of health. . . .[33]

Ford to Swift, November 6, 1733.

. . . I have long had it at heart to see your works collected, and published with care. It is become absolutely necessary, since that jumble with Pope, &c. in three volumes, which put me in a rage whenever I meet them. . . . I doubt you have been too negligent in keeping copies [of pamphlets] ; but I have them bound up, and most of them single besides. I lent Mr Corbet that paper to correct his Gulliver by ; and it was from it that I mended my own. There is every single alteration from the original copy ; and the printed book abounds with all those errors, which should be avoided in the new edition.

In my book the blank leaves were wrong placed, so that there are perpetual references backwards and forwards, and it is more difficult to be understood than the paper ; but I will try to get one of the second edition, which is much more correct than the first, and transcribe all the alterations more clearly. I shall be at a loss how to send it afterwards, unless I am directed to somebody that is going to Ireland. . . .[34]

Swift to Ford, November 20, 1733.

. . . I gave you an account in my last how against my will a Man here is printing the Works of &c by Subscription. Gulliver vexeth me more than any. I thought you had entred in leaves interlined all the differences from the originall Manuscript. Had there been onely omissions, I should not care one farthing ; but change of Style, new things foysted in, that are false facts, and I know not what, is very provoking. Motte tells me He designs to print a new Edition of Gulliver in quarto, with Cutts and all as it was in the genuin copy. He is very uneasy about the Irish Edition. All I can do is to strike out the Trash in the Edition to be printed here, since you can not help me. . . . It was to avoyd offence, that Motte got those alterations and insertions to be made I suppose by Mr Took the Clergyman deceased. So that I fear the second Edition will not mend the matter, further than as to litteral faults. For instance, the Title of one Chapter is of the Queens administration without a prime Minister &c, and accordingly in the Chapter it is said that she had no chief Minister &c: Besides, the whole Sting is taken out in severall passages, in order to soften them. Thus the Style is debased, the humor quite lost, and the matter insipid. . . .[35]

The story of Swift's connection with the Faulkner edition during the next year and a half can be pieced together, with some gaps, from Swift's correspondence and the preface to the edition itself.

Swift to Pope, July 8, 1733.

> As to the printing of my things going on here, it is an evil I cannot prevent. I shall not be a penny the richer. Some friends correct the errors, and now and then I look on them for a minute or two. But all things except friendship and conversation are become perfectly indifferent to me, and yet I wish this collection could have been made on your side, and if I were younger, it would be some mortification to have it as it is.[36]

Swift to the Earl of Oxford, August 30, 1734.

> As to the printer, all he has done or will do in the matter is against my will. Neither have I concerned myself further with him than to let him know that if he should publish anything offensive or unworthy, as mine, he should have cause to repent it. Further I could not go, for neither printers nor booksellers have any property here as in London. The man is very submissive, and I have no remedy but patience. He hath gotten several copies from my friends, which I suffered them several years ago to take, and I am forced to be passive in what is done with them. In London the things ascribed to me are in the hands of different proprietors, else I could have prevented this evil here. I have put the man under some difficulties by ordering certain things to be struck out after they were printed, which some friends had given him. This hath delayed his work, and as I hear, given him much trouble and difficulty to adjust. Farther I know not, for the whole affair is a great vexation to me.[37]

Publisher's Preface to the Faulkner edition, issued about March 1, 1734-5.

> ... the supposed Author's Friends ... were pleased to correct many gross Errors, and strike out some very injudicious Interpolations; particularly in the Voyages of Captain *Gulliver*: ... the supposed Author was prevailed on to suffer some Friends to review and correct the Sheets after they were printed; and sometimes he condescended, as we have heard, to give them his own opinion.[38]

Swift to William Pulteney, March 8, 1734-5.

> You will hear, perhaps, that one Faulkner hath printed four volumes, which are called my Works; he has only prefixed the

first letters of my name; it was done utterly against my will; for there is no property in printers or booksellers here, and I was not able to hinder it. I did imagine, that after my death, the several London booksellers would agree among themselves to print what each of them had by common consent; but the man here has prevented it, much to my vexation, for I would as willingly have it done even in Scotland. All this has vexed me not a little, as done in so obscure a place. I have never yet looked into them [i.e., the *published* volumes], nor, I believe, ever shall. . . .[39]

Swift to Pulteney, May 12, 1735.

You are pleased to mention some volumes of what are called my works. I have looked on them very little. It is a great mortification to me, although I should not have been dissatisfied if such a thing had been done in England by booksellers agreeing among themselves. . . . The printer applied to my friends, and got many things from England. The man was civil and humble, but I had no dealings with him, and therefore he consulted my friends, who were readier to direct him than I desired they should. . . .[40]

Swift to the Earl of Oxford, September 2, 1735.

I was indeed a little angry, but more grieved, to see four volumes called my Works printed at all in Ireland; but as the man assured my friends, and as it was generally known that some hedge printer would have done the like, and mix them with other people's trash, my friends advised him to it, and he submitted to all their corrections, and to leave out what they thought proper, for I could not hinder him.[41]

Swift to Motte, November 1, 1735.

Mr. Faulkner in printing those volumes did what I much disliked, and yet what was not in my power to hinder, and all my friends pressed him to print them, and gave him what manuscript copies they had occasionally gotten from me. My desire was, that those works should have been printed in London, by an agreement between those who had a right to them. I am, Sir, with great truth, . . .[42]

Swift to Motte, May 25, 1736.

Sir,

I lately received a long letter from Mr. Faulkner, grievously complaining upon several articles of the ill treatment he hath met with from you, and of the many advantageous offers he hath made you, with none of which you thought fit to comply. I am not qualified to judge in the fact, having heard but one side; only one thing I know, that the cruel oppressions of this kingdom by England are not to be borne. You send what books you please hither, and the booksellers here can send nothing to you that is written here. As this is absolute oppression, if I were a bookseller in this town, I would use all the safe means to reprint London books, and run them to any town in England, that I could, because whoever offends not the laws of God, or the country he lives in, commits no sin.

It was the fault of you and other booksellers who printed anything supposed to be mine, that you did not agree with each other to print them together, if you thought they would sell to any advantage. I believe I told you long ago, that Mr. Faulkner came to me, and told me his intention to print everything that my friends told him they thought to be mine, and that I was discontented at it, but when he urged, that some other bookseller would do it, and that he would take the advice of my friends, and leave out what I pleased to order him, I said no more, but that I was sorry it should be done here. But I am so incensed against the oppressions from England, and have so little regard to the laws they make, that I do, as a clergy-man, encourage the merchants both to export wool and woollen manufactures to any country in Europe, or anywhere else, and conceal it from the Custom-house officers, as I would hide my purse from a highwayman, if he came to rob me on the road, although England hath made a law to the contrary; and so I would encourage our booksellers here to sell your authors' books printed here, and send them to all the towns in England, if I could do it with safety and profit; because, I repeat it, it is no offence against God, or the laws of the country I live in. Mr. Faulkner hath dealt so fairly with me, that I have a great opinion of his honesty, although I never dealt with him as a printer or a bookseller; but since my friends told me those things, called mine, would certainly be printed by some hedge bookseller, I was forced to be passive in the matter.

I have some things which I shall leave my executors to publish after my decease, and have directed that they shall be printed in London; for, except small papers, and some treatises writ for the use of this kingdom, I always had those of importance to be published in London, as you well know. For my own part, although I have no power anywhere, I will do the best offices I can to countenance Mr. Faulkner; for, although I was not at all pleased to have that collection printed here, yet none of my friends advised me to be angry with him; although, if they had been printed in London by you and your partners, perhaps I might have pretended to some little profit. Whoever may have the hazard or advantage of what I shall leave to be printed in London after my decease, I will leave no other copies of them here; but, if Mr. Faulkner should get the first printed copy, and reprint it here, and send his copies to England, I think he would do as right as you London booksellers, who load us with yours. If I live but a few years, I believe I shall publish some things that I think are important; but they shall be printed in London, although Mr. Faulkner were my brother. I have been very tedious in telling you my thoughts on this matter, and so I remain, Sir,

Your most humble servant,

TO MR. BENJAMIN MOTTE,   JON. SWIFT.
BOOKSELLER, IN LONDON.[43]

Seventeen years after the publication of Faulkner's edition, and seven years after the death of Swift, the Earl of Orrery brought out his *Remarks on the Life and Writings of Jonathan Swift*. His account of the Dean's connection with the edition, if read with care, will be seen to confirm the picture already painted:

. . . there is no just, or perfect edition of [Swift's] works. Faulkner's edition, at least the first four volumes of it . . . were published by the permission and connivance, if not by the particular appointment of the Dean himself. . . .

The English edition of Swift's works I have scarce seen: and I have had little inclination to examine it, because I was acquainted with the Dean, at the time when Faulkner's edition came out, and therefore must always look upon that copy as most authentic; well knowing that Mr. Faulkner had the advantage of printing his edition, by the consent and approbation of the author himself. The first four volumes were published by subscription, and every sheet of them was brought to the Dean for his revisal and correction. The next two were published in the same manner.[44]

Orrery does, however, make two statements which appear to be inconsistent with each other. He refers to "the author (who was in reality the editor)":[45] but on the next page he says, "The situation and arrangement [of the minor works] was left entirely to the editor. In that point, the Dean either could not, or would not give him the least assistance." This is the first intimation that any one friend of the Dean had special responsibilities in connection with the edition: who he was is a matter to be discussed later.

The two statements by a contemporary of Swift which assign to the Dean a greater hand in the preparation of the Faulkner edition were both made by Faulkner himself. The first of these appeared in the *Dublin Journal* for September 29-October 2, 1744 (when Swift, because of mental incapacity, was unable to deny it). It stated that "the Author was pleased to consent, and was so kind as to correct the whole work, ready for printing."[46] The second statement was more circumstantial: it was made in reply to a series of criticisms of the Faulkner text by John Hawkesworth, who had been, since 1755, the editor of the London edition of the works published by Charles Bathurst. Faulkner's preface to his edition of 1768 is, therefore, the culmination of a publishers' war. In this preface Faulkner refers to "the Editor of this, and the other Editions" published by him, and avers that Swift had consented to the issuance of the edition of 1735 upon certain conditions:

That the Editor should attend him early every morning, or when most convenient, to read to him, that the Sounds might strike the Ear, as well as the Sense the Understanding, and had always two Men Servants present for this Purpose; and when he had any Doubt, he would ask them the Meaning of what they heard; which, if they did not comprehend, he would alter and amend until they understood it perfectly well, and then would say, *This will do; for I write to the Vulgar, more than to the Learned.* Not satisfied with this Preparation for the Press, he corrected every Sheet of the first seven Volumes that were published in his Life Time, desiring the Editor to write Notes, being much younger than the Dean, acquainted with most of the Transactions of his Life, . . .[47]

Several objections to this account present themselves at once. It was made by a man sixty-five years of age, nearly thirty-five years after the events it purported to describe.[48] It was made in self-interest as the last shot in a war with another publisher who had goaded Faulkner for thirteen years before eliciting this reply. It is inconsistent with Faulkner's own account, in his original edition, of Swift's relation to the project. Finally, it is not borne out by the nature of the emendations of *Gulliver's Travels* which appeared in the Faulkner edition, none of which can be said to have been motivated by a desire to make the book more comprehensible to the vulgar. If the statement has any value, it is probably as a description of Swift's method of writing or revising certain Irish tracts such as the *Drapier's Letters.*

The statements of Orrery and Faulkner suggest that among the various friends who assisted Swift in preparing the 1735 edition one was sufficiently predominant to be regarded as "the editor." The men most likely to have held this post were Patrick Delany, Thomas Sheridan, and Orrery himself. Sheridan died in 1738, and hence could not have been the editor of the later Faulkner editions. Orrery survived until 1762, and Delany until 1768. Either of the two latter, therefore, might have prepared the 1772 edition of the *Travels*, which constitutes the third volume of a set of which the first volume is dated 1768. The gap between 1762 and 1768 makes Orrery less likely to have been the "editor": moreover, when work on the first Faulkner edition was begun in 1733, Orrery was about twenty-six or twenty-seven years of age, and had known Swift only two years. Delany, at that time, was about forty-eight, and had been a friend of Swift since 1718. All in all, the probabilities are in his favor.[49]

Before embarking on a detailed comparison of the texts of 1726 and 1735 it is important to settle, if possible, the basic text from which Swift and his friends worked in preparing the Dublin edition. It will be remembered that Ford offered, if he could, to correct a copy of the "second" edition (by which he meant the fourth octavo, 1727) and send it to Swift, because his own annotated copy of the first edition had the interleaved corrections in the wrong places, and because the "second" edition was more nearly accurate than any other.[50] This was true in so far as Motte had followed the minor emendations suggested in Ford's letter to him, but there were, of course, new minor errors which had crept into the fourth octavo when it was printed. The fact that almost none of these new minor errors occur in the 1735 text indicates that Ford did not carry out his intention. Further evidence of this may be found in the "advertisement" which Faulkner printed at the beginning of his edition of the *Travels*:

> We are assured, that the Copy sent to the Bookseller·in London, was a Transcript of the Original, which Original being in the Possession of a very worthy Gentleman in London, and a most intimate Friend of the Authors; after he had bought the Book in Sheets, and compared it with the Originals, bound it up with blank Leaves, and made those Corrections, which the Reader will find in our Edition. For, the same Gentleman did us the Favour to let us transcribe his Corrections.[51]

The only loophole that the most captious could find in this forthright statement is the possibility that Ford had made up a second interleaved copy, preferring not to let the original out of his hands. There are at least two other annotated copies in existence which appear to have been made up either by Ford himself or by someone who had access to his corrections.[52] But as the corrections used in the Faulkner edition come closer to Ford's annotated copy than to these others, the facts seem reasonably free from doubt.

The text of *A Letter from Capt. Gulliver to his Cousin Sympson* presents its own problem. Faulkner, whose edition is now the sole source for it, printed it as a preface, though in intention it is a postscript. It is dated April 2, 1727, but a number of scholars have held that it was really written expressly for Faulkner.[53] The reasons advanced for this theory

are that this is an instance of Swift's love of "mystification";
that in 1727 he would not have said that seven months had
elapsed since the *Travels* were published (the true period
being a little more than five months) ; that at the end of April,
1727, Swift was carrying on negotiations with Motte about
the *Travels*, without reference to this letter; and that if the
letter had been sent to Motte he would not have parted with
it in 1735 for the benefit of a rival publisher.

With regard to the supposed purpose of "mystification," it
is hard to imagine what difference it would have made to the
public whether the letter was dated 1727 or 1735. The slip
in the dates may have come about either because Swift (who
was, of course, not in England when the book was published
in October) may have been absentmindedly harking back to
the month of August, when he left the book in the hands of
his English friends; or he may have been mentally counting,
"October, November, December, January, February, March,
April—seven months." I cannot see why Swift should not
have continued negotiations with Motte after sending him
this letter. The final argument—that Motte would not have
given up the letter for Faulkner's benefit—rests upon two
assumptions: that Swift actually sent the letter to Motte and
that he kept no copy. As the letter was not very long, the
second assumption seems unwarranted. And Swift may never
have sent the letter to Motte. Just five days after April 2,
1727, Swift wrote to Thomas Tickell requesting a license to
leave Ireland for six months.[54] This letter bears the marks of
haste: the decision to go abroad seems to have been suddenly
arrived at. It is not at all improbable that Swift, having composed the letter to Motte, decided not to send it until he had
had a chance to visit England and talk to the publisher at first
hand. One positive argument in favor of the date as it stands
is the similarity, in content and in phraseology, of Ford's
letter to Motte of January 3, 1727, and the Sympson letter—
a similarity much easier to explain if only three months had
intervened between the two.[55]

The collations which follow may seem tedious, but they
are unavoidable, containing, as they do, much important

internal evidence bearing on the relative reliability of the Motte and the Faulkner texts. They are divided into three sections: variant readings which involve differences in meaning; variants concerned with grammar and idiom; and purely stylistic variants. The first section is the longest, the most detailed, and, of course, the most significant.

REFERENCES to *Gulliver's Travels* here, as elsewhere, are to book, chapter, and paragraph. Motte's four octavo editions are designated as 01, 02, 03, and 04 (the "second edition, revised" of 1727). Faulkner's edition, in his *Works* of 1735, is cited as *W*. The first reading of each passage quoted is that of 01, unless otherwise indicated. *Ford* refers to Charles Ford's annotated copy of the first edition.

ALTERATIONS IN MEANING

INSTANCES IN WHICH THE READING OF THE 1735 WORKS IS PREFERABLE

2.1.8. I . . . laid my self at Length upon the Handkerchief . . .
   W   I . . . laid my self at full length . . .
The reading of *W* removes the ambiguity.

2.3.11. [The dwarf] seldom failed of a small Word upon my Littleness.
   W   . . . a smart Word . . .
The improvement is obvious.

2.5.12. . . . my Coat . . . being made of that Country Cloth . . .
   W   . . . that Country Silk . . .
The Queen (2.3.7) had ordered that Gulliver's clothes be made of the country's thinnest silk. The emendation is intentional, and shows unusual vigilance, whether made by Swift or another.

2.8.9. He said, they saw my Stick and Handkerchief thrust out of the Hole, and concluded, that some unhappy Men must be shut up in the Cavity.
   W   . . . some unhappy Man . . .
The second reading is more logical.

3.5.14.　We crossed a Walk to the other part of the Academy, where, as I have already said, the Projector in speculative Learning resided.

　　　W　. . . the Projectors . . .

This has the appearance of a misprint overlooked by Ford.

3.5.17.　He assured me, that this Invention had employed all his Thoughts from his Youth, that he had employed the whole Vocabulary into his Frame . . .

　　　W　. . . he had emptyed the whole Vocabulary . . .

Motte's printer carelessly repeated "employed" from the preceding line.

3.8.9.　Returning back to his own Vessels . . .

　　　W　. . . Vessel . . .

The commander had been in charge of one ship only.

3.9.1.　. . . we sailed in the River *Clumegnig*, which is a Sea-port Town . . .

　　　W　. . . the River of *Clumegnig* . . .

Perhaps another misprint overlooked by Ford.

3.10.11.　That, this Breed of *Struldbruggs* was peculiar to their County . . .

　　　W　. . . to their Country . . .

An obvious misprint in the first edition.

3.10.18.　[The struldbruggs] are deprived and hated . . .

　　　W　. . . are despised and hated . . .

Ford failed to note this slip: it was, however, corrected in a pirated Dublin edition of 1726 and in Motte's octavo edition of 1727.

4.2.3.　. . . I saw three of these detestable Creatures, whom I first met after my Landing

　　　W　. . . Creatures, which I first met . . .

The emendation is clearly correct, since it agrees with Gulliver's invariable attitude toward the yahoos as beasts.

INSTANCES IN WHICH THE READING OF
THE FIRST EDITION OR OF FORD'S EMENDATION
IS PREFERABLE

Table of contents, 2.7 and 4.11. These differ from the corresponding chapter-headings in the 1735 edition. In the first case the

sentence, *"The King's great Ignorance in Politicks."* is omitted:
in the second the reading is *"The Author arrives at Europe."*
instead of *"The Author arrives at England."*

1.1.5. ... One of their largest Hogsheads ... did not hold half
a Pint ...
    W ... hardly held half a Pint ...
Hogsheads used for beer or ale in eighteenth-century England
usually contained forty-eight gallons, those used for wine
sixty-three. Taking the latter size as the "large Hogshead,"
and dividing its content by 1728^{56} to reduce it to the Lilliputian
scale, we get $7/24$ of a pint, which agrees with the wording of
the first edition, but not with that of Faulkner's, since "hardly
held" implies that the contents of the hogshead closely approx-
imated half a pint.

1.2.3. [The emperor] kept without the length of my Chain.
    W ... of my Chains.
At first sight the 1735 reading seems to be superior, since
Gulliver had said (1.1.10) that he was held captive by "four-
score and eleven Chains." But more careful investigation re-
veals that throughout the second chapter the set of chains is
regarded as a single instrument of confinement and is therefore
referred to in the singular. In the other three places where the
chain is mentioned in this chapter (1.2.2, twice, and 1.2.10)
the *Works* retain the singular of the first edition. In 1.3.20,
when Gulliver describes his release, the unlocking of the
numerous padlocks requires a reversion to the plural form,
which is accordingly used in both editions.

1.2.7. ... on the transparent side [of Gulliver's watch] we saw
... Figures ... and thought we could touch them, till we found
our Fingers stopped by that lucid Substance.
    W ... stopped with that lucid Substance.
"Stopped with," in the English idiom of 1726, as in that of the
present day, meant "filled with," not "arrested by."

1.3.5. ... a fiery Horse that belonged to one of the Captains
pawing with his Hoof struck a Hole in my Handkerchief, and
his Foot slipping, he overthrew his Rider and himself; but I
immediately relieved them both, and covering the Hole with one
Hand, I set down the Troop with the other, in the same manner
as I took them up.

W . . . For covering the Hole . . .

The alteration seems to have been made to avoid a repetition of "and," as well as to prevent the beginning of a clause with that conjunction: these two principles of style will be discussed later. Their application here, however, results in an illogical change of sense. The original passage represents Gulliver as first picking up the fallen horse and rider, and then, in fear of further accidents, removing the rest of the troop: the 1735 version makes him relieve the captain and his horse by lifting down the whole troop.

1.5.1.   I walked towards the North-East Coast over against *Blefuscu*, and lying down behind a Hillock . . . viewed the Enemy's Fleet . . .

W   I walked to the North-East Coast . . .

Gulliver had previously avoided appearing on the coast for fear of being seen by the Blefuscudians. "Towards" is therefore the more precise word here.

1.6.14 : 1.6.16.   The Nurseries for [male] Children of ordinary Gentlemen, Merchants, Traders, and Handicrafts, are managed proportionably after the same manner; only those designed for Trades, are put out Apprentices at Eleven years old, whereas those of Persons of Quality continue in their Nurseries till Fifteen, which answers to One and Twenty with us; but the Confinement is gradually lessened for the last three Years.

W   . . . are put out Apprentices at seven Years old . . .

In the Nurseries of Females of the meaner sort, the Children are instructed in all kinds of Works proper for their Sex, and their several degrees: those intended for Apprentices, are dismissed at nine Years old, the rest are kept to thirteen.

W   . . . dismissed at seven Years old, the rest are kept to eleven.

Hubbard argues as follows in favor of the 1735 emendations:

"In brief, according to both Motte and Faulkner, the boys and girls of 'Quality' go home on the attainment of their majority, which is at fifteen and twelve years respectively. According to Motte, the boys apprenticed leave at eleven, and the girls apprenticed at nine, the other girls of the 'meaner' sort being kept until thirteen, one year beyond the attainment of their majority.

"The usual period of apprenticeship in England was probably seven years. Seven years 'with us' are equivalent to five years in Lilliput, so far at least as males are concerned, which is evident from a comparison of the ages of majority ($21:15 = 7:5$). It is also contrary to a sound principle of law to apprentice a person for a term of years extending beyond the age of majority. Hawkesworth and the Motte text violate this principle when they adopt eleven years as the beginning of apprenticeship for boys, and the Motte text when it adopts nine years for girls; and prolong this service in the one case to sixteen years for boys, and in the other to fourteen years for girls.

"The above changes in the Faulkner text are not accidental. The boy-apprentices serve from seven to twelve, the girls from seven to twelve, and the other, 'meaner,' girls are dismissed at eleven; none of them beyond the age at which they attain their majority."[57]

This argument is based upon two misapprehensions. In the first place, Swift calls twelve not the age of majority for Lilliputian girls, but "the marriageable Age" (1.6.15). In the second place, it was not contrary to law in 1726 to apprentice a child for a term of years extending beyond the age of majority: on the contrary, the Statute of Artificers (1562) *required* that apprentices should be bound until they reached the age of twenty-four. Many gilds buttressed this legal requirement by their own rules. The Statute remained in force until 1767. The apprenticeship of girls always ended at majority (twenty-one years) or on marriage. The purpose of the original law, of course, had been to assure the apprentice a thorough training before he had to shift for himself.[58]

With these facts in mind, let us translate the ages involved in the passages under discussion, remembering that Swift prefers not to deal in fractions, but to use the whole number nearest to the age he intends.

Expressed in European terms, the ages for apprenticeship, according to the first edition, are fifteen for boys and twelve for girls: since the *minimum* legal period of apprenticeship in England was seven years, presumably the boys would serve until they were at least twenty-two, and the girls until they were at least nineteen. The "meaner" girls who were not apprenticed would be dismissed from training at eighteen.

On the other hand, if the ages given in Faulkner's edition are translated into English equivalents, we find both boys and girls being apprenticed at ten—a fact which Hubbard seems not to have considered. Cases of children being put to work at this age, or even younger, were not unknown in 1726, but the best trades set twelve to fourteen years as a minimum.[59] If, therefore, we adopt the readings of the Faulkner edition we represent Swift as approving conditions of child labor less humane than those which were actually in existence in the best trades in England in his own day.

1.6.15. ... neither did I perceive any Difference in their Education [that of Lilliputian young ladies as compared with that of Lilliputian young gentlemen] ... only that ... a smaller Compass of Learning was enjoined them: for, the Maxim is, that among People of Quality, a Wife should always be a reasonable and agreeable Companion, because she cannot always be young.

W ... For, their Maxim is ...

The relative pronoun substituted for the article in the 1735 edition seems to refer to the preceding "them," i.e., the young ladies: Swift meant that the maxim was a general belief of the Lilliputians.

1.8.1. ... I went back the shortest way ...

W ... the shorted Way ...

An obvious misprint.

2.1.2. ... we ... brought the Ship to.

W ... brought the Ship too.

A misprint.

2.1.2. We got the Star board Tacks aboard ...

W ... the Star-board Tack ...

This passage occurs in the description of a storm which Swift copied from Sturmy's *Mariner's Magazine*.[60] The first edition follows Sturmy in reading "Tacks," which is, of course, nautically correct: the word here means "ropes," not the course of the ship, as the 1735 text implies.

2.2.3. My Master ... took along with him his little Daughter my Nurse upon a Pillion behind him.

W ... upon a Pillion behind me.

Probably a printer's error.

2.3.8.   [The Queen] put a Bit of Bread in her Mouth, as big as two twelve-penny Loaves.

    W   ... twelvepenny Loves.

A misprint.

2.3.9.   ... his first Minister, ... near as tall as the Main-mast of the Royal *Soverain* ...

    W   ... as tall as the Main-most ...

Another misprint.

2.4.3.   [Lorbrulgrud] contains above eighty thousand Houses, and about six hundred thousand Inhabitants.

    W omits and about six hundred thousand inhabitants.

As the subject of this paragraph is the populous character of the country, and Lorbrulgrud is chosen as an example of the cities, the omission of the interesting detail from the 1735 edition looks like carelessness on the part of the printer. This can hardly be a case of omission to avoid repetition, as seven lines intervene between "inhabited," which occurs in the earlier part of the paragraph, and "inhabitants," and in any event the infelicity could have been remedied by changing the latter word to "persons."

2.8.2.   ... I attended the King and Queen in a Progress to the South Coast ...

    W   ... in Progress to ...

"A progress" means a formal royal visitation. Possibly Faulkner's printer did not understand the expression.

2.8.2.   On the Roof of my Closet, not directly over the middle of the Hammock, I ordered the Joyner to cut out a Hole ...

    Ford   ... Closet, just over ...

    W   ... Closet, set not directly over ... I order ...

Ford's correction, from the original manuscript, is presumably made because Gulliver could not have reached the hole conveniently except from the hammock. The change from "ordered" to "order" in 1735 is doubtless a misprint.

2.8.5.   I was not able to lift up the Roof of my Closet, which otherwise I certainly should have done, and sate on the top of it, where I might at least preserve my self some Hours longer than by being shut up, as I may call it, in the Hold.

    W   ... I might preserve myself from being shut up ...

The alteration makes the latter part of the sentence fatuous.

3.1.3. [The captain] gave me power to Traffick for two Months, while he transacted his Affairs at *Tonquin*.
    W omits for two Months.
The phrase dropped from the 1735 text is not redundant: it represents the captain's estimate of the time within which Gulliver should return in order not to delay the main expedition. Probably the omission was accidental.

3.3.14-18. *Ford* About three years . . . change the Government.
    W omits these five paragraphs describing the rebellion of Lindalino.
Faulkner evidently felt that this important passage was still too dangerous for an Irish publisher to bring out under his own imprint.

3.5.8. . . . Acorns, Dates, Chesnuts, and other Maste . . .
    W . . . and other Masts . . .
"Mast," the collective noun meaning the fruit of beech, oak, and other forest trees, was never used in the plural until the nineteenth century, and then only rarely. The plural form in the eighteenth century meant "spars" only: see OED, "mast."

3.6.12. *Ford* . . . [the decipherers] can discover a Closestool to signify a Privy Council, . . . a Codshead a ———, . . . a Buzzard a prime Minister, . . . a Sink the Court . . .
    W omits a Codshead a———*and* prime, *and reads* a Sink, a C———t.
All three alterations are obvious softenings of the satire on the English court. This is another example of Faulkner's prudence.

3.7.3. [The governor] hath . . . a Park of about three thousand Acres. . . . In this Park are several smaller Inclosures for Cattle, Corn, and Gardening.
    W . . . several small Inclosures . . .
The inclosures for cattle and grain were presumably not positively small, but only comparatively smaller than the park. Hubbard suggested that the change was made by a compositor who wished to save a line.

3.11.4. We landed at a small Port-Town called *Xamoschi*, situated on the *South-East* part of *Japan*; the Town lies on the *Western* Point where there is a narrow Streight, leading *Northward* . . .

W . . . the Town lies on the *Western* Part . . .

Not only does this presumably unintentional change introduce a repetition of a word, contrary to one of Swift's principles of style, but it renders the geographical description less clear.

4.1.4. [The female yahoos] had long lank Hair on their Faces, nor any thing more than a sort of Down on the rest of their Bodies . . .

Ford . . . lank hair on their Heads, but none on their Faces, nor . . .

W . . . lank Hair on their Heads, and only a Sort of Down . . .

The reading of the original manuscript, supplied by Ford, was intended to mark the difference between male and female yahoos, and thus to emphasize the physical parallel with human beings.

4.1.4. . . . I ran to the Body of a Tree. . . . Several of this cursed Brood . . . leapt up in the Tree, from whence they began to discharge their Excrements on my Head: However, I escaped pretty well, by sticking close to the Stem of the Tree . . .

W . . . sticking close to the Stem of a Tree . . .

A misprint.

4.2.1. There were [in the first room of the Houyhnhnm's house] three Nags, and two Mares, not eating, but some of them sitting down upon their Hams, which I very much wondered at; but wondered more to see the rest employed in domestick Business. They seemed but ordinary Cattle; however this confirmed my first Opinion, that a People who could so far civilize brute Animals, must needs excel in Wisdom all the Nations of the World.

W The last seemed but ordinary Cattle; . . .

The 1735 text distinguishes between the three nags and the two mares, on the one hand, and the rest of the horses in the room on the other, and implies that only the latter were servants. This is incorrect, as appears from the following paragraph, which places the members of the family in an inner room apart from the servants.

4.3.10. I expressed my uneasiness at his giving me so often the Appellation of *Yahoo*, an odious Animal, for which I had so utter an Hatred and Contempt, . . .

W ... the Appellation of *Yahoo,* and odious Animal, ...
Clearly a misprint: Swift did not mean that Gulliver's master
had called him "odious Animal."

4.4.2. I owned, that the *Houyhnhnms* among us, whom we
called *Horses*, were . . . when they belonged to Persons of
Quality, employed in Travelling, Racing, or drawing Chariots ...
W ... Travelling, Racing, and drawing Chariots ...
The first edition makes clear the fact that horses in Europe
were employed according to their abilities.

4.4.6. ... others fled for ... Murder, ... flying from their
Colours, or deserting to the Enemy, ...
W ... deserting the Enemy ...
The omission of "to" reverses the real meaning of the passage.

4.6.5. *Ford* ... Birds, Beasts and Fishes ...
W ... Beasts and Fishes ...
The ignoring of Ford's correction was probably a slip on the
"editor's" part.

4.7.7. That in some Fields of his Country, there are certain
shining Stones of several Colours, whereof the *Yahoos* are
violently fond, and when Part of these *Stones* is fixed in the
earth, as it sometimes happeneth, they will dig with their Claws
for whole Days to get them out, ...
W ... when Part of these *Stones* are fixed in the
Earth, ...
Swift's meaning was that a part of each individual stone to
which he refers was imbedded, not that some stones were
partly buried in the earth and others were lying loose upon it.

4.7.10. ... there was nothing that rendered the *Yahoos* more
odious, than their undistinguishing Appetite to devour every
Thing that came in their way ...
W ... their undistinguished Appetite ...
Almost certainly a compositor's error.

4.7.11. There was also another kind of *Root* very *juicy*, but
somewhat rare and difficult to be found, which the *Yahoos* sought
for with much Eagerness ...
W ... the *Yahoos* fought for ...
The statement in the first part of the sentence regarding the
difficulty of finding the root makes it practically certain that

the reading of the first edition is right, and that this is one of the instances (surprisingly rare) in which a compositor misread a long *s* as an *f*.

4.7.11. . . . they would howl and grin, and chatter, and tumble, and then fall asleep . . .

> *Ford* . . . and chatter, and reel, and tumble . . .
> *W* . . . and chatter, and roul, and tumble . . .

Ford's correction from the manuscript follows closely the successive steps of intoxication in the yahoos. The 1735 alteration (possibly accidental) misses a step, and introduces a redundancy in "roul, and tumble."

4.8.8. Having lived three Years in this Country . . .

> *W* Having already lived three Years . . .

The reason for this confusing emendation is explained below in connection with another alteration in 4.11.10.

4.8.14. . . . my Master thought it monstrous in us to give the Females a different kind of Education from the Males, except in some Articles of Domestick Management; whereby as he truly observed, one half of our Natives were good for nothing but bringing Children into the World: And to trust the Care of our Children to such useless Animals, he said was yet a greater Instance of Brutality.

> *W* . . . to trust the Care of their Children to such useless Animals . . .

The shift in emphasis caused by the altered pronoun is very undesirable: it does not seem so heinous to permit mothers to care for their own children.

4.8.15. Four times a Year the Youth of a certain District meet to show their Proficiency in Running, and Leaping . . .

> *W* . . . the Youth of certain Districts . . .

The first version means that each district holds contests for its own youth: the second, that there are contests in some districts, but not in others.

4.10.2. . . . his Honour, to my great Admiration, appeared to understand the Nature of *Yahoos* in all Countries, much better than myself. He went through all our Vices and Follies, and discovered many which I had never mentioned to him, by only supposing what Qualities a *Yahoo* of their Country, with a small portion of Reason, might be capable of exerting.

W omits in all Countries.

The omitted phrase is vital to the meaning: Gulliver would not have been surprised at his master's understanding the yahoos of Houyhnhnmland. The second sentence clinches the matter.

4.10.4. When I thought of . . . my Countrymen, or Human Race in general, I considered them as they really were, *Yahoos* in Shape and Disposition, only a little more civilized, and qualified with the Gift of Speech, but making no other use of Reason, than to improve and multiply those Vices, whereof their Brethren in this Country had only the share that Nature allotted them.

W . . . Disposition, perhaps a little more civilized . . .

"Perhaps" was clearly substituted for "only" in order to avoid repetition. The substitution introduces an undesirable change in the sense: there was no doubt in the minds of the Houyhnhnms or of Gulliver that the latter was superior to the yahoos of Houyhnhnmland in civilization. The proper emendation would have been "disposition, except that they were . . ."

4.11.7. . . . and then their Country [Portugal] and ours [England] were at Peace.

W . . . their Country and ours was at Peace.

The alteration in the number of the verb makes the English and the Portuguese citizens of a common country.

4.11.10. . . . my three Years' Residence [in Houyhnhnmland].

W . . . my five Years' Residence . . .

This emendation and that in 4.8.8 were intended to remedy a supposed inconsistency with Gulliver's statement that he had come from England about five years before he was found by the Portuguese sailors (4.11.7). But the emendations are errors: whoever made them forgot that by no means all of Gulliver's absence from England was passed in Houyhnhnmland. He had sailed from Portsmouth in August or September, 1710 (4.1.1), but had not been marooned until May 9, 1711 (4.1.3): he departed from Houyhnhnmland on February 15, 1714-15 (4.11.1). The interval was three years, nine months and six days.

4.11.11. The Captain . . . at last began to have a better Opinion of my Veracity, and the rather because he confessed, he met with a *Dutch* Skipper, who pretended to have landed with Five others of his Crew upon a certain Island or Continent *South* of *New-*

Holland, where they went for fresh Water, and observed a Horse driving before him several Animals exactly resembling those I described under the Name of *Yahoos*, with some other Particulars, which the Captain said he had forgot; because he then concluded them all to be Lies.

W omits all of this sentence after Veracity.

This deletion was undoubtedly made to avoid a supposed conflict with Gulliver's statement (4.12.9), "no *European* did ever visit these Countries before me." But the difficulty had been foreseen in the beginning: Gulliver had continued, "I mean, if the Inhabitants ought to be believed." In other words, the Dutch sailors, if they actually had visited the island, had not been seen by the Houyhnhnms.

4.12.9.   I am ready to depose . . . That no *European* did ever visit these Countries before me. I mean, if the Inhabitants ought to be believed; unless a Dispute may arise about the two *Yahoos*, said to have been seen many Ages ago on a Mountain in *Houyhnhnmland*, from whence the Opinion is, that the Race of those Brutes hath descended; and these, for any thing I know, may have been *English*, which indeed I was apt to suspect from the Lineaments of their Posterity's Countenances, although very much defaced. But, how far that will go to make out a Title, I leave to the Learned in Colony-Law.

W omits unless a Dispute . . . Colony-Law.

Hubbard suggested that this was struck out because the satire on the English was too savage.[61] Such a tenderness would hardly have been characteristic of Swift. It seems more probable that the passage was deleted under the mistaken impression that it called attention to an inconsistency: cf. the discussion of the passage omitted from 4.11.11.

DEBATABLE EMENDATIONS

1.2.6.   . . . a Person of great Quality, who was looked upon to be as much in the Secret as any . . .

W . . . who was as much in the *Secret* . . .

The revised form is more forthright, but the original is characteristic of Gulliver's caution about overstating facts.

1.2.10.   When this Inventory was read over to the Emperor, he directed me, although in very gentle Terms, to deliver up the several Particulars.

W omits although in very gentle Terms.

Hubbard thought that the suppression of the phrase "restores the full authority of command accorded the emperor in the rest of this interview."[62] On the other hand, it weakens the ludicrous effect which Swift achieves here and elsewhere by making the gigantic Gulliver express respectful admiration at the condescension and good nature of the monarch.

1.6.18. . . . Begging is a Trade unknown in this Kingdom.

    W . . . in this Empire.

As Lilliput is an empire, the substituted word is more accurate: but "Kingdom" and "Empire" are used interchangeably elsewhere in the voyage, and the 1735 text is emended only in this passage.

1.7.14. . . . to strew a poisonous Juice on your Shirts, which would soon make you tear your own Flesh . . .

    W . . . on your Shirts and Sheets, which . . .

The change, though probably intentional, adds nothing of importance.

2.1.9. . . . a small Dram-cup, which held about three Gallons . . .

    W . . . about two Gallons . . .

The eighteenth-century dram (when the term was used in connection with liquor) was half a gill, or one eighth of a pint. Multiplying this by 1728 to find the Brobdingnagian equivalent, we get twenty-seven gallons instead of three. The emendation of 1735 is therefore in the wrong direction, but the figures in both editions are very far from accuracy. Swift (like Newton's printer) may have dropped a zero in his calculations, and have arrived at two and seven tenths, instead of twenty-seven; more probably, he was in this instance concerned with the amusing picture he was drawing, rather than with mathematical accuracy, just as he was in the case of the troop of cavalry which exercised on Gulliver's handkerchief.

2.3.4. [The Queen] took me in her own Hands, and carried me to the King. . . . I lay upon my Breast in her Majesty's right Hand.

    W . . . took me in her own Hand, . . .

The emendation is not really necessary for consistency: if it was intentional it shows remarkable vigilance.

2.3.6. One of these Virtuosi [the King's scholars] seemed to think . . .

 W One of them seemed to think . . .

Perhaps the term "Virtuoso" was falling into disuse in 1735, but it is retained at 4.10.1.

2.5.8. . . . the Head [of the executed criminal], when it fell on the Scaffold Floor, gave such a bounce, as made me start, although I were at least half an *English* Mile distant.

 W . . . at least an *English* Mile . . .

The Brobdingnagian "scale" is not involved here, and the change seems pointless: quite possibly it was accidental.

2.5.13. Here I sat for some time three hundred Yards from the Ground . . .

 W . . . five Hundred Yards . . .

The extra height may have been added to increase the feeling of Gulliver's peril. Hubbard, however, remarked that the ladders which were raised would, in European terms, have been impractical in length according to the 1735 reading—125 feet, as contrasted with 75 feet in the original edition.[63] Still, the ladders need not have been raised from the ground level.

2.7.3. I . . . could direct his Workmen how to make [cannon], of a Size proportionable to all other Things in his Majesty's Kingdom, and the largest need not be above an hundred Foot long . . .

 W . . . need not be above two hundred Foot long . . .

Reduced to European scale, these cannon would be either eight feet four inches or sixteen feet eight inches in length. Cannon of the smaller size were in common use in 1726 and, as Gulliver is here attempting to minimize the difficulty of the project he is proposing, the reading of the first edition is perhaps better.

2.7.11. A *Cavalier* mounted on a large Steed might be about an hundred Foot high.

 W . . . about Ninety Foot high.

Here the 1735 text decreases the size instead of increasing it. The two heights, expressed in European figures, are respectively eight feet four inches and seven feet six inches. Hubbard estimated the height of an average trooper on an average horse (sixteen hands high) at eight feet one inch, and noted

that "a large steed might make the measurements of the first
edition approximately correct."[64]

3.2.10.   . . . the Husband is always so rapt in Speculation . . .
    W   . . . wrapped in Speculation . . .
The general idea is unaffected by the change: the compositor
may have regarded this as merely a different spelling.

3.3.9.   . . . Glasses far excelling ours in Goodness. For this
Advantage hath enabled them . . .
    Ford   . . . Goodness. For although their largest Telescopes
    do not exceed three Feet, they magnify much more than
    those of an hundred Yards among us, and at the same time
    shew the Stars with greater Clearness. This Advantage . ∴ .
    W   . . . Goodness. For, although their largest Telescopes
    do not exceed three Feet, they magnify much more than
    those of a Hundred with us, and shew the Stars with greater
    Clearness. This Advantage . . .
Telescopes of a hundred feet or a hundred yards were alike in-
conceivable to the eighteenth-century mind. There seems to be
no reason for the slight verbal changes from Ford's manuscript
version.

3.6.12.   *Ford*   . . . Informers . . . all under the Colours and
Conduct of Ministers of State and their Deputys . . .
    W   . . . under the Colours, the Conduct and pay of Min-
    isters . . .
The addition is intentional and strengthens the satire to some
extent.

3.6.12.   *Ford*   It is first agreed . . . what suspected persons shall
be accused of a Plot: then effectual Care is taken to . . . put the
Criminals in Chains.
    W   . . . put the Owners in Chains.
Perhaps the "editor" felt that "criminals," which was used
ironically, might be misconstrued.

3.8.4.   Neither could I wonder at all this, when I saw such an
Interruption of Lineages by Pages, Lacqueys, Valets, Coachmen,
Gamesters, Captains, and Pick-pockets.
    W   . . . Gamesters, Fidlers, Players, Captains, . . .
The additions may have been imported into the passage from
the more elaborate catalogue in 4.10.1, where pickpockets,
gamesters and fiddlers also appear. The alteration is, as Hub-

bard remarks, characteristic of Swift, and may have come from his hand.[65]

3.9.4. But this good Prince was so gracious, as to forgive the poor Page [who had maliciously compassed the death of a young lord] his Whipping, upon promise that he would do so no more, without special Orders.

   W omits poor.

The deletion is quite possibly a printer's error. The omitted word pointed up the delightfully ironic misdirection of the reader's sympathy.

4.1.5. . . . raising up his right Forefoot to remove my Hand.

   W . . . his Left Fore-Foot . . .

There is no apparent reason for this change, unless it be the repetition involved in the phrase "right hoof" seven lines later.

4.3.9. He then stroaked my Body very gently . . . after which he said . . . that I differed very much from the rest of my Species, in the Softness, and Whiteness, and Smoothness of my Skin . . .

   W omits Softness, and

Apparently an accidental omission, unless it was felt that softness and smoothness were qualities so much alike as to make the first version redundant.

4.4.1. . . . that Faculty of *Lying*, so perfectly well understood among human Creatures.

   W . . . understood, and so universally practised among . . .

The added words make the sentence more specific, but also a little banal.

4.5.2. . . . a Hundred or more Cities taken, and thrice as many Ships burnt or sunk.

   W . . . and five times as many Ships . . .

In the absence of accurate statistics it is impossible to prefer one set of figures over the other.

4.5.4. . . . Land, that would render our Dominions round and compleat.

   W . . . round and compact.

The general sense is unchanged, though the words are not exactly synonymous. There is no apparent reason for the emendation.

4.5.12. *Ford* First, my Lawyer . . . is quite out of his Element when he would be an Advocate for Justice, which as an Office unnatural, he always attempts with ill Will.

    W . . . with great Awkwardness, if not with Ill-will.

The addition introduces a new idea, but seems to weaken the satire.

4.5.13. *Ford* . . . the Judges never fail of decreeing accordingly.

    W . . . of directing accordingly.

As there is no mention of juries, the former word seems to be more accurate.

4.5.17. [lawyers] were the most ignorant and stupid among us . . .

    W . . . were usually the most ignorant . . .

Once again the satire is weakened.

4.7.11. . . . and then fall asleep in the Dirt.

    W . . . in the Mud.

The emendation might be thought both more accurate and more repellent.

4.7.15. . . . such Degrees of Brutality . . .

    W . . . such Degrees of infamous Brutality . . .

The intensification seems a little redundant.

4.8.16. *Ford* [At the representative council of the whole nation it is determined] when a Child hath been lost . . . what Family in the District shall breed another to supply the Loss.

    W omits in the District.

Probably an unintentional overlooking of Ford's correction.

4.10.1. . . . I did not find the Treachery or Inconstancy of a Friend . . .

    W . . . I did not feel the Treachery . . .

The second version reads more naturally, but by implication alters the sense: the meaning now seems to be that Gulliver experienced these misfortunes, but did not mind them. A better emendation would have been: "I did not undergo . . ."

4.10.2. . . . Where the greatest *Decency* was observed . . .

    W . . . where (as I have already said) the greatest . . .

This addition, as it does not affect either the sense or the emphasis of the passage, is of no essential importance. As Hubbard observed, however, it is characteristic of Swift, and shows remarkable alertness on the part of the person who made it, since the previous reference to decency occurred in 4.8.10.[66] It is even more remarkable, considering Swift's failing powers of memory at this period, if he was responsible for the emendation.

4.12.9. *Ford* ... I did humbly conceive [that those countries were not proper fields for colonization by England]. However, if those whom it more concerns, think fit to be of another Opinion ...
    W ... if those whom it may concern, think fit ...
The contrast is made more clearly in the earlier version.

ALTERATIONS IN GRAMMAR AND IDIOM

IN eighteen instances the 1735 edition changes indicatives to subjunctives. Two of the alterations are for the better:

3.10.12. It supposed a Perpetuity of Youth, Health, and Vigour, which no Man could be so foolish to hope, however extravagant he may be in his Wishes.
    W ... however extravagant he might be ...

4.12.3. I could heartily wish a Law was enacted ...
    W ... a Law were enacted ...

In seven cases the change to the subjunctive is undesirable, if not positively wrong: these are all instances of clauses beginning with "though" or "although." For example:

Preface. Although Mr. Gulliver was born in Nottinghamshire ...
    W Although Mr. Gulliver were born ...

2.8.6. This gave me some faint hopes of Relief, although I was not able to imagine how it could be brought about.
    W ... although I were not able to imagine ...

In the remaining instances either the indicative or the subjunctive would be correct, and the chief effect of the change is to make the speaker seem a little more precise of speech—

perhaps a little too precise for a sea-captain. One case of the erroneous change from subjunctive to indicative in the 1735 edition should be noted:

3.5.11. . . . this being repeated three or four times, the adventitious Wind would rush out, . . . and the Patient recover.
    W . . . and the Patient recovers.

There are about a dozen changes of tense between the editions: a few are worth comment:

2.1.4. I durst not stay to see the Issue of that Adventure, but ran as fast as I could . . .
    W . . . but run as fast as I could . . .

2.6.16. [whether gamesters might not force nobles] by the Losses they have received, to learn and practice that infamous Dexterity upon others.
    W . . . by the Losses they received . . .

2.8.2. I ordered the Joyner to cut out a Hole . . .
    W . . . I order the Joyner . . .
Only the second of these emendations is correct.

3.6.12. *Ford* I told him, that in the Kingdom of Tribnia . . . the Bulk of the People consist . . . of Discoverers. . . . The Plots in that Kingdom are . . .
    W . . . the Bulk of the People consisted . . .

4.6.10. I told him, that a . . . *Minister of State* . . . is a Creature wholly exempt from Joy . . .; at least makes use of no other Passions but a violent Desire of Wealth . . . ; That he applies his Words to all Uses . . . ; That he never tells a Truth . . .
    Ford . . . was a Creature . . . at least made use of . . .
    W . . . was a Creature . . . at least makes use of . . .
In the first instance Ford's emendation is correct: in the second his alterations cause the shift in tenses to occur at a less awkward place than Faulkner's. The failure to make both changes in 1735 was probably an oversight.

4.4.2. I owned, that [horses in Europe] were treated with much Kindness and Care, till they fell into Diseases. . . . But the common Race of Horses had not so good Fortune, being kept by

... mean People, who put them to greater Labour, and fed them worse.

    W ... and feed them worse.

4.6.11. ... these *Ministers* ... preserve themselves in Power ..., secured themselves from after Reckonings, and retired ...

    W ... secure themselves ... and retire ...

The second 1735 emendation is right.

Four times the 1735 edition changes the number of a verb:

1.2. (heading). *The Emperor of* Lilliput, *attended by several of the Nobility, come to see the Author* ...

    W ... *comes to see the Author* ...

3.5.11. ... the Bellows were full of Wind ...

    W ... the Bellows was full of Wind ...

4.6.1. That the Bulk of our People were forced to live miserably, by labouring every Day ...

    W ... was forced to live miserably ...

4.8.11. *Ford* ... some other couple bestow him one of their own Colts ...

    W ... bestows on him one of their own Colts ...

In the first case the alteration is undoubtedly right. The other three involve the preference for a single or a plural verb after a collective noun. In the first of these either would be permissible. In the second, however, it is the individual person, not the bulk, that labors, and the plural verb of the first edition is better. In the last case there is no doubt: if the "editor" changed "bestow" to "bestows" he should also have changed "their" to "its."

Closely related to these alterations of the number of verbs are four other cases involving the number of nouns or pronouns:

1.6.10. ... whoever makes ill Returns to his Benefactor, must needs be a common Enemy to the rest of Mankind, from whom he hath received no Obligation ...

    W ... from whom they have received no Obligation ...

2.6.4. [The sticks] were thicker at one end than the other, and I covered the thicker ends with a piece of Mouse's Skin, that by rapping on them, I might neither damage the tops of the Keys, nor interrupt the Sound.

    W   . . . I covered the thicker End . . .

3.5.19.   We next went to the School of Language, where three Professors sate in Consultation upon improving that of their own Country.

    W   . . . School of Languages . . .

4.9.7.   They have a kind of Tree, which . . . loosens . . . and falls with the first Storm; they grow very strait, and being pointed like Stakes . . . they stick them erect in the ground . . .

    W   . . . it grows very strait . . .

In the first of these cases the 1735 version is clearly wrong: in the third the emendation is preferable to the original. In the other two instances the editor, in trying to improve two loosely constructed sentences has failed to carry through his corrections, and has left confusion worse confounded.

In five passages the editions disagree as to the use of "or" or "nor": in the first, third, and fourth of these the edition of 1735 is correct:

1.6.11.   [The bringing of a child into the world] was neither a Benefit in itself, or intended so by his Parents . . .

    W   . . . nor intended . . .

3.2.1.   . . . they can neither speak, nor attend to the Discourses of others . . .

    W   . . . or attend to the Discourses . . .

4.1.4.   . . . I never beheld . . . so disagreeable an Animal, nor one against which I naturally conceived so strong an Antipathy.

    W   . . . or one against which . . .

4.3.4.   He was sure no *Houyhnhnm* alive could make such a Vessel, nor would trust *Yahoos* to manage it.

    W   . . . or would trust *Yahoos* to manage it.

4.10.5.   [The assembly had said] That such a Practice was not agreeable to Reason or Nature, nor a thing ever heard of before . . .

    W   . . . or a thing ever heard of before . . .

The 1735 edition once substitutes "will" for "shall," and once "would" for "should." The first emendation is probably, though not certainly better: the second is wrong:

Preface (paragraph 5).   . . . if any Traveller hath a Curiosity to see the whole Work at large . . . I shall be ready to gratify him.
   W   . . . I will be ready . . .

3.5.9.   And he proposed farther, that by employing Spiders, the Charge of dyeing Silks should be wholly saved . . .
   W   . . . would be wholly saved . . .
There are perhaps twenty-five other miscellaneous grammatical slips which occur in one of the two editions but not in the other. Some of these may be permissible eighteenth-century idioms: others may be due to carelessness on the part of the printer. A few examples will suffice:

1.1.5.   I heard a knocking . . . like that of People at work.
   W   . . . like People at work.

1.3.6.   . . . as I was entertaining the Court with these kind of Feats . . .
   W   . . . these Kinds of Feats . . .

1.3.9.   . . . the *Man-Mountain*, lately arrived to our Celestial Dominions . . .
   W   . . . arrived at our Celestial Dominions . . .

2.2.2.   . . . what an Indignity I should conceive it to be exposed for Money as a publick Spectacle . . .
   W omits it.

2.3.11.   [The dwarf] became insolent at seeing a Creature so much beneath him, that he would always affect to swagger . . .
   W . . . became so insolent . . .

3.6.7.   Wit, Valour, and Politeness were . . . to be largely Taxed . . . by every Persons giving his own Word for the Quantum of what he possessed . . .
   W   . . . by every Person giving his own Word . . .

4.1.4.   . . . they had . . . Claws before and behind, terminating in sharp points . . .
   W   . . . terminating on sharp points . . .

4.6.4.　But that Nature . . . should suffer any Pains to breed in our Bodies, he thought it impossible.

W omits it.

4.10.1.　I often got Honey out of hollow Trees, which I mingled with Water, or eat with my Bread.

W . . . or eat it with my Bread.

ALTERATIONS IN STYLE

THE most interesting group of stylistic emendations in the *Travels* is connected with Swift's conception of Gulliver's character. The hero was intended to be a little old-fashioned in both morals and speech, and the author seems to have been uncertain of the degree to which the latter quality should be emphasized. In the manuscript used by Motte, for example, the older form of the possessive was used consistently in the phrases "mine Eyes" and "mine Ears." Ford's letter to Motte corrected these to "my Eyes" and "my Ears," except in three instances which he overlooked. How the older forms got into the printer's copy is not clear. Possibly Swift used them in his original draft, changed his mind about them, and ordered the amanuensis who made the (hypothetical) final manuscript to make the alterations, only to have his instructions ignored or forgotten. A few other words are modernized in the edition of 1735: "through," for example, is substituted for "thorough" in the one instance where the latter word is used in its old sense; "sate" consistently becomes "sat," and "scape" is spelled "escape." The obsolescent word "Stang" (1.2.1), meaning a quarter of an acre, is allowed to remain, however, as is the sea-language which Gulliver, in his *Letter to Sympson*, said the modern sea-yahoos found out of date. As if in partial balancing of these changes, the 1735 edition in more than twenty cases reverts to the slightly archaic third person singular verb form ending in *th* instead of *s*—hath, doth, maketh. Swift used some of these forms in his correspondence to the end of his life, and perhaps he felt that they imparted the precise flavor that he wanted. The changes are not made with absolute consistency, however, and in one instance the alteration results in a palpable error. This is in the description of the cryptographers of Tribnia (3.6.13). In the cipher sentence, *"Our Brother Tom has just got the Piles,"* "has" is changed to "hath": this spoils the anagram. Whoever was responsible for this, whether Swift or one of his friends, either forgot or had never realized that the anagram was genuine.

A desire to avoid the repetition of words or phrases was responsible for the largest group of emendations in the 1735 edition. Swift's friends were acquainted with this principle of his, as appears from the list of corrections Ford sent to Motte. Many, perhaps most of the changes made for this reason were improvements. A few examples will illustrate the range:

1.2.3. [The Emperor] surveyed me round with great Admiration, but kept without the length of my Chain.
W . . . kept beyond the Length . . .

1.5.6. . . . wherewith I shall not trouble the Reader. . . . [fourteen lines omitted] . . . but shall not trouble the Reader with the Particulars.
W . . . but shall not interrupt the Reader . . .

1.6.14. The Nurseries for Children of ordinary Gentlemen . . . [three lines omitted] . . . whereas those of Persons of Quality continue in their Nurseries . . . [three lines omitted] . . . In the female Nurseries . . .
W . . . continue in their Exercises . . .

The principle is extended in two cases to similarities of sound:

3.6.3. This Project could not be of any great Expence to the Publick, and would, in my poor opinion, be of much Use . . .
W . . . and might in my poor Opinion . . .

4.4.4. . . . it is impossible to represent his noble Resentment . . .
W . . . it is impossible to express . . .

Frequently, however, the emendations are unskillfully made: there is no attempt to recast a sentence or a paragraph completely, and as a consequence the revised text is inferior to the original. Sometimes a change alters the sense or the emphasis:

1.4.4. He . . . added, that if it had not been for the present Situation . . . perhaps I might not have obtained [my liberty] so soon. For, said he, as flourishing a Condition as we may appear to be in to Foreigners, . . .
W . . . as flourishing a Condition as we appear to be . . .

As the courtier who is speaking is merely inferring the conclusions of Gulliver about Lilliput, the original is right.

3.8.7. . . . for these [vices] I gave, as was reasonable, great
Allowance.
    W . . . I gave, as it was reasonable, due Allowance.
The change was made because "greatness" occurred two lines
later: it makes the sentence rather fatuous.

3.8.9. . . . [the command of the ship] was given to a Youth
who had never seen the Sea . . .
    W . . . was given to a Boy . . .
"Youth" had occurred twice earlier in the same paragraph, at
distances of six and thirteen lines. "Boy," however, is a poor
substitute, as it makes the commander implausibly young.

Sometimes the emendation introduces a new repetition, or
ignores one far more serious than that which is being altered.

2.1.5. [The stile] had four Steps, and a Stone to cross over
when you came to the uppermost. It was impossible for me to
climb this Stile, because every Step was six Foot high, and the
upper Stone above twenty.
    W . . . when you came to the utmost. . . .
Not only is "utmost" a bad synonym for "uppermost," but in
this paragraph "stile" occurs four times in fourteen lines, and
"stone" twice in three.

2.6.10. *Ford* This Conversation was not ended under five
Audiences, each of several Hours, and the King heard the whole
with great Attention, frequently taking Notes of what I spoke,
as well as Memorandums of several Questions he intended to
ask me.
    W . . . Memorandums of what Questions . . .
The repetition of "several" is avoided at the expense of re-
peating "what," which occurs in the line immediately preceding. There are also three cases (2.7.8; 4.2.2; 4.8.1) in which
repetitions are introduced into the text by emendations for
which there is no ostensible reason.

Redundancy does not appear to have been a fault which
concerned the editor of the 1735 text greatly, for while some
cases of it are cured, new ones spring up:

1.7.23. It was a Custom . . . that after the Court had decreed any cruel Execution . . . the Emperor made a Speech . . .
    W . . . *inserts* always *before* made a Speech.

2.3.8. I had an entire Set of Silver Dishes . . . which in Proportion to those of the Queen, were not much bigger than what I have seen of the same kind in a *London* Toy-shop . . .
    W omits of the same kind.

4.6.14. One Day in Discourse my Master . . . was pleased to make me a Compliment . . .
    W omits in Discourse.

4.7.9. . . . which my Master would needs contend to have some kind of Resemblance with our *Suits at Law* . . .
    W omits kind of.

4.11.1. . . . considering . . . that the Wind might chop about . . .
    W adds probably *after* might.

Twenty-two times "though" is changed to "although" in the 1735 text, and twelve times "till" becomes "until." The latter series of changes is the more striking, because, while Swift in his other writings used "though" and "although" indiscriminately, he seems to have had a strong preference for "till" rather than "until." Since plenty of instances of "till" remain in the Faulkner edition, it is quite possible that compositors were responsible for the dozen changes.

The remaining stylistic emendations are of small importance. Three colloquial contractions (t'other, 'em [twice], and 'Tis) are expanded in 1735. A few examples will show the miscellaneous character of the other minor alterations:

1.2.6. His Answer, as I could apprehend it, was . . .
    W . . . as I could apprehend, was . . .

1.4.4. . . . on account of his Quality, and Personal Merits, as well as the many good Offices he had done me . . .
    W . . . as well as of the many good Offices . . .

3.4.12. . . . he must . . . destroy all his Plantations, and cast others in such a Form as modern Usage required . . .
    W . . . cast others into such a Form . . .

3.6.12.   *Ford* . . . to fill their Pockets with Forfeitures . . .
    W   . . . to fill their Coffers . . .

3.7.4.   . . . he hath a Power of calling whom he pleaseth . . .
    W   . . . he hath Power of calling . . .

The history of the 1735 text, as it emerges from this mass of internal and external evidence, is clearer than might have been expected. Swift, who had been hoping for an English collected edition of his works, greeted the Irish project with considerable distaste, but grudgingly gave it a limited support. So far as *Gulliver's Travels* was concerned he was chiefly anxious to see the major "murdered pages" restored (he never speaks of revising, but only of getting the correct readings from the original manuscript). The corruption of the text which annoyed him most was that which described Queen Anne as not having made use of a prime minister: since the first voyage was an allegorical account of the Tory ministry of Oxford and his second in command, Bolingbroke, it is easy to understand Swift's anger. To further the printing of a correct version Swift sought and obtained from Ford the nearest available substitute for the original manuscript: but he was unable to persuade Faulkner to print some political references in their most pungent form, and one important incident, referring to "Wood's brass pence," was regarded by the printer as too dangerous to use at all. The details of the edition Swift delegated in large part to friends, particularly to one unidentified person (possibly Patrick Delany) whom Orrery and Faulkner call "the editor." These friends read proof in the form of sheets which Faulkner was required to submit for approval: they made emendations in accord either with their own ideas or with general principles laid down by Swift, who from time to time worked with them and undoubtedly made some alterations of his own. It is, however, impossible to identify these. In the end, when the volumes were finally off the press, Swift seems to have been disinclined to look at them.

The number of demonstrable errors in meaning is far greater in the 1735 text than in the original as corrected by Ford. A number of these errors show that whoever made them, whether Swift or another, either had never known or had forgotten[67] the reasons underlying the original version. Many of the emendations in grammar and style are improvements, but others show a lack of thoroughness, and some even affect the sense adversely. There are also new grammatical errors and stylistic infelicities in the 1735 edition which indicate carelessness on the part of those in charge, and there are so many minor variations in unimportant details as to make it clear that the compositors and proofreaders in Faulkner's shop were much less conscientious than those in Motte's.

The 1735 text, then, is a composite and relatively untrustworthy piece of editing. It is true that a number of its variant readings may have come from Swift's pen, but it is impossible to identify them. It is also true that many of the other intentional variants were made by Swift's general permission. This, however, is beside the point. In law *qui facit per alium facit per se*, but not in literature. The text of 1726 as amended by Ford's careful comparison with the original manuscript, on the other hand, is universally agreed to be as close as is humanly possible to the book as its author intended it to be at the close of a six-year period of inspired creation and detailed revision. It is incomparably the best basis for a text of *Gulliver's Travels*.

The Geography and Chronology of Gulliver's Travels

SURPRISINGLY little attention has been paid by editors and commentators to the geography and chronology of *Gulliver's Travels*. Sir Henry Craik, in his *Selections from Swift*, found the geography worth a fairly extended passage,[1] Mr. G. R. Dennis, in his edition of *Gulliver*,[2] commented on some of the cruces, and Mr. Harold Williams devoted some space in the introduction of his edition to a discussion of the maps.[3] Mr. Williams also provided his readers with the most satisfactory commentary we possess on the difficulties and inconsistencies of the time-scheme.[4] The conclusions reached by these scholars, and, indeed, by almost all students of Swift who have occupied themselves with the problem, were that Swift worked out for his book a detailed framework in time and space, but that it is (at least as it has come down to us) so imperfect that it is impossible to reconcile it with itself or to be sure, in many instances, of the author's intentions. Recently, however, Professor John R. Moore has suggested that the geography and chronology of the *Travels* are so nonsensical as to indicate intentional confusion: in other words, they are part of a satiric burlesque of travel literature.[5]

Undoubtedly the framework of the *Travels* presents difficulties. Unless some happy chance brings to light more material like the Ford letters we shall have to rely on conjectures with regard to a number of points. Yet it is possible to solve a good deal of the puzzle, and to come much closer to certainty than is usually believed.

Two geographical authorities are spoken of in the *Travels* —Nicolas Sanson and Herman Moll. The only mention of the former is found in the second voyage, where the "little Book" carried by Glumdalclitch is described (2.2.8) as "not much larger than a *Sanson's Atlas*." There is nothing to indicate that Swift ever looked inside the covers of this book, which he cites only because it is the largest he can think of. There was, indeed, little reason for using Sanson as an authority. His atlases had all been published in the seventeenth century, and the first quarter of the eighteenth had seen great advances in geographical knowledge, especially in the neighborhood of those regions in which Swift was to place his imaginary countries. Swift's obvious course was to avoid, as far as possible, any gross contradictions of accepted cartography, and he could not have effected this more surely and easily than by following the maps of Moll. This eminent English engraver of Dutch extraction had industriously gathered geographical data from the turn of the century, and by Englishmen, at least, his maps were widely accepted as the standard. As a matter of fact, however, the early eighteenth-century maps were much of a muchness, at least so far as the general physical structure of the world was concerned. Even in the regions of the South Seas (a term which sometimes included the North as well as the South Pacific) the cartographers tended to agree, only venturing to show occasional divergences in minor details, and often attempting to hedge by the use of faintly drawn coast lines which warned the reader not to put too much faith in what was, at best, unverified information.

Swift's remarks about Moll are entirely different in tone from his incidental reference to Sanson. Gulliver ventures (4.11.3) to disagree respectfully with Moll in the matter of the southeastern portion of New Holland, which is, he insists, at least three degrees west of the position it occupies in Moll's maps. This is enough to show that Swift had consulted Moll with attention: it also shows that he felt it safe, in the current state of geographical knowledge, to dispute minor points even with an expert. Whether he relied on any other sources it is impossible to say. No atlas appears in the catalogue of his library as it existed at the time of his death, but he did own numerous books of travel, most of which contained charts of some kind.[6] Among them was Dampier's *New Voyage around the World* (1697) which, it is almost certain, Swift read intensively. This book contains some of Moll's earliest maps, including one of the world, and another of the Netherlands East Indies and the northern part of New Holland or Australia. Some of the place names Swift uses in the *Travels* differ in form from those used by Moll: but these Swift may have taken from the mass of travel literature which he read during the period in which the book was composed.[7] In any event, a fairly extensive search among the maps and atlases of the period has brought to light no map which agrees more closely than Moll's with Gulliver's geography, and it will be convenient to use the former's *A New & Correct Map of the Whole World* (1719) as a basis for discussion.[8]

Swift's primary geographical problem was not a difficult one. He had to find, in the unexplored portions of the globe, locations for seven imaginary countries, only two of which were of considerable size. It was desirable that these locations should not be so close to either pole as to be obviously unfit for human habitation, and Swift apparently felt also that they should not be too close to the equator: the climates do not seem to differ much from that of England. It was also necessary to take care that these countries did not lie too close to each other, or to trade routes generally known to Europeans, though, on the other hand, they could not lie too far from these routes, lest it should be difficult to account for Gulliver's arrivals and departures. Accordingly we find that the three smallest countries, Lilliput, Blefuscu, and Houyhnhnmland, are placed not far from Australia, although on different sides, and that Brobdingnag, Balnibarbi, and the islands described in the third voyage are situated in the North Pacific, by far the largest area which remained unexplored by Europeans in 1720.

An examination of Moll's map shows the astuteness of Swift's choices.[9] Most traders with the Orient in the eighteenth century preferred to hug the coast line of Asia, sailing to China through the multitudinous islands which lie between Siam and Australia. Consequently the Malay Archipelago was well known to mariners, save for New Guinea, the eastern and southern coasts of which were in dispute, some cartographers boldly uniting the island with Australia, while others remained noncommittal. The northern and western coasts of Australia had been determined with considerable accuracy, but the eastern and southeastern shores were not even guessed at, although there was a general agreement that it was possible to sail between Australia and New Zealand, the southwestern corner of which appears in Moll's maps. Exploration in the North Pacific had been checked by the disinclination of the Japanese to deal with Europeans: even the Dutch, who had a monopoly of occidental trade with Japan, had for nearly a century been limited to the port of Nagasaki. There was, therefore, almost no knowledge of the geography of northern Japan and of the regions which lay beyond. It was not known how far Iesso (Yezo) extended, whether it was an island or a peninsula, or whether any lands lay to the north or the east of it, although many maps vaguely indicated a territory to the east called "Company's Land"—claimed by the Dutch East India Company on the ground of explorations early in the seventeenth century. This land was separated from Yezo by the "Straits of the Vries," which led to a hypothetical northwest passage to Europe, hope for the discovery of which had not yet been abandoned. The eastward extent of "Company's Land" was frankly a matter of conjecture, some maps indicating only the western tip, others showing (though in faint lines) a coast stretching almost due east to within a short distance of the North American coast, close to the "Straits of Annian." Western North America was perhaps the most mysterious region of all. The cartographers were not even sure whether California was an island or a part of the main continent. Many maps, including Moll's, showed the Gulf of California extending northward until it rejoined the Pacific at the entrance to Puget Sound, north of Cape Blanco. San Francisco Bay was undiscovered, and to the north and west of Puget Sound lay a perfect and absolute blank.

With so much of the globe at his disposal it would seem that Swift should have had no trouble in arranging his hypothetical countries without coming into too violent conflict with accepted geography. And yet a series of misfortunes has led to a very general misunderstanding of his intentions. The chief misfortune was the fact that Swift, because of the secret method employed to publish the *Travels*, was unable to read proof and correct errors of detail. It is impossible to determine to what extent the errors were the fault of the author, the transcriber, and the printer, but that there were errors is undeniable. The second misfortune was that the maker of the maps for the original edition was careless or stupid or both. He was guilty of mistakes for which there can be no excuse—the misspelling of names, the miscalculation of comparative distances, the misplacing of localities with respect to each other when there was no discrepancy in the text from which he worked. But despite all this, and despite the fact that no one believes that Swift approved the maps, certain assumptions which the original engraver made have been accepted by modern scholars without question, with the result that Swift has been charged with errors of which he was not guilty. The engraver's practice seems to have been to read the text until he came to the first description of the location of the land Gulliver was visiting, then to assume that this description was accurate, and that any conflicting supplementary data must be reconciled with it, or ignored, if reconciliation proved to be impossible. It seems never to have occurred to him to assemble all of the geographical data in a given voyage, to try to harmonize the whole and, if conflicts appeared, to seek a solution of the difficulty without giving preference to any statement because it came early in the tale rather than late. And yet such a procedure would have prevented a series of blunders which begins with the first voyage.

The wreck which cast Gulliver upon the shores of Lilliput occurred "Northwest of *Van Diemen's* Land" and "in the Latitude of 30 Degrees 2 Minutes South" (1.1.5). Two areas bear the name "Van Dieman's Land" (or "Dimen's Land") in eighteenth-century maps—northwestern Australia and Tasania—but as the former lies between ten and twenty degrees outh latitude it cannot have been intended here by Swift nless the passage in the *Travels* is hopelessly corrupt. But ere are difficulties even if one assumes that the reference is o Tasmania. A glance at a modern map will reveal what was pparent to the eyes of the engraver of the original maps for e *Travels*: that a point northwest of Tasmania and in lati- ude 30° 2′ S. lies not in the ocean but well inland in Australia. timid soul might have solved this discrepancy by moving illiput a little to the south of Australia, in latitude 32° or 3° S. The engraver was made of bolder stuff. He moved asmania some forty-five degrees to the west, and placed illiput in the Indian Ocean, due south of the western end of umatra. Australia was ruthlessly erased from the map. It is ot surprising to find that this was only the beginning of the ngraver's liberties. Both Lilliput and Blefuscu are drawn n a scale far too large, as compared with Sumatra, and Iildendo appears as "Mendendo."

Yet after all this manipulation of the facts there are more ifficulties to come. When Gulliver left Blefuscu he sailed rst north and then northwest (1.8.9). "My Intention," he ays, "was to reach, if possible, one of those Islands, which had reason to believe lay to the North-East of *Van Die- 1en's* Land." On the third day he was picked up about twenty- our leagues from Blefuscu, in latitude 30° S., by a ship sail- ng on a southeasterly course in its return from Japan "by he *North* and *South-Seas*." Either an eighteenth- or a twen- ieth-century map will show the ridiculousness of this account f we assume that Lilliput lies either south of Sumatra, as Iotte's engraver thought, or in the Great Australian Bight, s some later commentators have suggested. It represents Gulliver as attempting to sail entirely around Australia in earch of an island on which to land, and it describes the ship's aptain as laying a southeasterly course from the neighbor- ood of Sumatra in order to reach England. If we adopt the heory which seems to be most favored today—that Van Diemen's Land is northwestern Australia, and that the posi- ion of Lilliput is about 15° S. and 120° E., similar difficulties

arise: they can be solved only by supposing that the islan
Gulliver was searching for lay northwest of Australia, an
that the ship which rescued him was on a southwesterly cours
—in other words, by changing the text in four places i
order to achieve a result which is uncertain and unsatisfa
tory.

In all the speculation about this crux it does not seem t
have occurred to anyone to question the accuracy of the firs
datum of all. Yet if one supposes that Lilliput lies north*ea*.
of Tasmania, instead of north*west* of it, all difficulties vanisl
The position thus indicated lies in the South Pacific abou
midway between Brisbane and the North Cape of New Zea
land. Gulliver's project of sailing northwest from Blefusc
in the hope of reaching an island northeast of Tasmania i
seen to be a thoroughly practicable plan, and the ship captain'
southeasterly course is recognized as entirely normal, sinc
traveling from the Orient to England by sailing aroun
Australia was an accepted alternative to following the shorte
but more difficult route through the Netherlands East Indie:
This solution disposes of all difficulties so simply and con
pletely that there can be little doubt of its correctness.

The geography of Brobdingnag is a much less complicate
matter. Even Motte's engraver was right as to its approxi
mate location, though he was characteristically careless in hi
scale, making the country far too small. Brobdingnag is
peninsula joined to the northern portion of the North Amer
ican continent (2.4.1). Gulliver's observation (2.4.2) that i
is "terminated to the North-east by a Ridge of Mountains
suggests that the main axis of the peninsula runs from south
west to northeast. The dimensions of the country (in whic
Swift is a little more generous than the map will allow) ar
"six thousand Miles in Length, and from three to five i
Breadth." The most helpful data about the location are give
in the last chapter of the voyage. The eagle which capture
Gulliver carried him fifty leagues from the coast (presumabl
the southern coast) of Brobdingnag, and dropped him some
where near 44° N. 143° E. According to Moll's map this posi
tion is just off the coast of Yezo, in the "Straits of the Vries.

This would fix one part of the southern coast of Brobdingnag in the vicinity of 45° N. 143° E., though the southernmost tip may lie some distance further to the southeast. A coast line running west-northwest and east-southeast may be extended as far as 20° N. 170° W. without interfering with either Moll's geographical data or the lands described in the third voyage, as their positions are worked out hereafter. From this point the eastern coast line may tentatively be carried north-northeast to 40° N. 140° W., and thence in a still more northerly direction to 70° N. 90° W., from which point the high mountain range which, according to Gulliver, separates Brobdingnag from the rest of North America, may be supposed to run northwest. The coast line, however, must be pure conjecture, since we are given only enough information to locate the points of Gulliver's arrival and departure, which lie very close to each other. The storm at the beginning of the second voyage caught the crew of the *Adventure* just east of the Moluccas, about three degrees north of the equator, and drove them a long distance east-northeast, after which a strong west-southwest wind carried them about five hundred leagues to the east. Such a course could easily have brought them to a position off the southern coast of Brobdingnag if it lay in the region suggested above. No doubt the point at which the landing was made was east of Flanflasnic, which seems to have been close to the southwest tip of the country. Such a location, of course, disposes of the hypothetical "Company's Land," but Swift would have felt no compunction over depriving the Dutch of territory.

It has been remarked that the dimensions of Brobdingnag are too large to be fitted into the map of the world as known to the eighteenth century.[10] The exaggeration was not, after all, very serious. The southern coast, as described above, would have given the country a width of three thousand miles, which might have been increased, farther up the peninsula, to well over four thousand. If the North American shore line above Cape Blanco bent backward to the east, so that the dividing mountain range was on the far side of the pole, a long axis of a good deal more than five thousand miles might be secured. Swift may, of course, have been careless in his calculations: he may even have been deceived as to the area at his disposal because he used a flat map instead of a globe. Most probably, however, he was not so much concerned with precise geography here as he was with providing the Brobdingnagians with a country suitable to their size: note, in the same passage, the mountains thirty miles high. In the first voyage Swift had ignored his scale deliberately for the sake of a picturesque incident—the troop of cavalry exercising on his handkerchief—and this slighter deviation for a more important purpose would probably not have worried him. If this is the case, however, it is pertinent to inquire why he chose just these dimensions as adequate for a country of giants. If one divides them by twelve, in accordance with the scale, they become five hundred miles in length and from two hundred and fifty to four hundred sixteen and two-thirds miles in breadth. The long axis of the British Isles, from Cape Wrath to the Isle of Wight, is about five hundred and sixty miles. The greatest width, taken at right angles to this axis, is from Bray Head, in Ireland, to Scarborough, about four hundred and fifty miles; elsewhere the width is commonly between two and three hundred miles. The figures are at least suggestive.

There is, however, one difficulty about the geography of Brobdingnag which becomes manifest only at the beginning of the third voyage. Here we learn (3.1.8) that Gulliver was boarded by pirates in the neighborhood of "the Latitude of 46 N. and of Longitude 183" (that is, 177° W.). This point, if previous calculations are correct, lies within the boundaries of Brobdingnag. But there are several good reasons for suspecting that the bearings thus given are inaccurate. In the first place, even if this position did lie within the ocean, it would have been an odd spot for eighteenth-century pirates to lurk about in search of prey. In the second place, it is hard to see how Gulliver's sloop could have reached this place by the course he describes. Finally, the bearings are inconsistent with the movements of Gulliver during the remainder of the third voyage. We have once more to do with an initial error which has been accepted without question, and which has consequently darkened counsel.

Motte's engraver outdid himself. He began by placing Balnibarbi (which he makes an island rather than a part of a continent) in latitude 43° N., a few hundred miles due east of Yezo. He was then confronted with the information (3.7.1) that Luggnagg lies northwest of Balnibarbi, and that this island, in turn, lies southeast of Japan. Lest there should be any doubt about this last point, Gulliver gives the exact position of Luggnagg—29° N. 140° E. The engraver compromised: he drew Luggnagg *south*west of Balnibarbi, so that it lay southeast of the northernmost part of Japan, and a good ten degrees east of the position given by Gulliver. His confusion of mind led him to commit the additional errors of attaching the island of Glubbdubdrib to Luggnagg, and placing the port of Maldonada in the latter island as well.

The process of working backward from data given late in the voyage produces, however, a clear and consistent picture. To begin with, the position of Luggnagg is described so circumstantially, and agrees so well with Gulliver's description of his voyage from thence to Japan, that we may feel ourselves on fairly safe ground. Balnibarbi is to the southeast of Luggnagg, and at a considerable distance from it, since Gulliver's voyage between the two countries occupied a month. Still, the length of the voyage was due in part to unfavorable winds, and perhaps we should look for the port of Maldonada in the neighborhood of 24° N. 149° E. This port is situated on the southern or western coast of Balnibarbi, since the island of Glubbdubdrib lies southwest of it. Lagado is about a hundred and fifty miles from Maldonada, and apparently south of it. Now the island from which Gulliver was rescued by the Laputans was ninety leagues (about three hundred and fifty miles) southwest by west of Lagado (3.2.8), and consequently about four hundred and fifty miles southwest by south of Maldonada, if the previous suppositions have been correct. By this reasoning Gulliver was marooned near 20° N. 145° E. —a long way from 46° N. 177° W. Which of these positions agrees more closely with Gulliver's account of his movements before he encountered the pirates?

Three days out of Tongking on a trading voyage, Gulliver's sloop was caught in a storm which drove it for five days, first northeast and then east, after which the weather became fair, but with a strong gale from the west for ten days. It is clear that the only northing the ship made occurred during the first part of the five days' storm. It is equally clear that no storm could drive a sailing vessel twenty-five degrees northward (more than sixteen hundred miles, even if the ship had no eastward motion) in five days. The commonly accepted position for Balnibarbi, east of Yezo, is an impossible one.

Once more, then, it is necessary to follow Gulliver's story with a map before us, in order to discover what Swift really intended. The Gulf of Tongking is a partially enclosed body of water from which Swift desired Gulliver to be carried into the Pacific. The storm which bore the sloop first northeast and then east (3.1.4) was designed to bring it first opposite Hainan Strait and then eastward through that passage into the open ocean. A ship on such a course would be following the twentieth parallel closely: ten days' progress due east with a strong following gale, partly of storm force, might easily bring it to 144° E. (a run of about thirteen hundred miles), although the precise longitude of the scene of the capture of the sloop may have been a few degrees east or west of this position. That the latitude was not far from 20° N. seems almost certain. How the erroneous "Latitude of 46. N. and of Longitude 183" found its way into the text it is impossible to explain: it may be an overlooked detail surviving from an early draft; it may be a mere error of transcription or a printer's mistake.

The final geographical problem, although it is the simplest of all, has nevertheless led to differences of opinion. In this case the customary geographical details are wanting at the beginning of the voyage, and calculations must be based on a brief passage near the end (4.11.3). From this we learn that Gulliver surmised that Houyhnhnmland lay west of New Holland (Australia), and about 45° S. He therefore decided to sail due east, in the hope of coming either to the southwest coast of Australia, or to some island to the west of that continent. To his surprise, two days' sailing brought him to the south*east* point of Australia. Dennis assumed that this was a mistake for southwest,[11] and in this opinion he has been followed by other commentators. The last part of Gulliver's account, however, confirms the reading of the original text. To begin with, the southwestern point of Australia is approximately 34° S., not 45° S. More important is the fact that if this had been the region intended, the geography would require further revision. After rounding the cape which he had first reached, Gulliver saw the ship which eventually rescued him approaching from the north-northeast (4.11.6)—a patent impossibility by either eighteenth- or twentieth-century maps if Gulliver had been near the southwestern tip of Australia. What Swift really meant was that Gulliver had reached the southern point of Tasmania, which, on Moll's map, lies about 44° S., about half a degree further south than it does in actual fact. Swift, in this passage, commits himself on two points which had not been finally determined by eighteenth-century cartographers : that Tasmania was joined to Australia, and that its southern extremity was "at least three Degrees" west of the location shown on Moll's map. Houyhnhnmland, therefore, lies a short distance due west of the southern tip of Tasmania, at about 44° S. 142° E. Motte's engraver was less at fault than usual in placing it at about 40° S. 125° E.

THE foregoing geographical scheme for *Gulliver's Travels* requires only two alterations in the text of the first edition. The time-scheme of the book is more detailed, and cannot be straightened out quite so easily, though the serious difficulties are confined to the third voyage. The second and fourth voyages are extremely simple. There is a slight slip at the beginning of the second. Gulliver returned from Blefuscu on April 13, 1702, and, as he remarked in the last paragraph of the first book, he sailed away again after two months. The actual date of his departure, as we learn from the first paragraph of the voyage to Brobdingnag, was June 20, but in the same paragraph his stay in England is given as ten months. The discrepancy was corrected by Motte in the fourth octavo, though Ford failed to note it in his emendations. The same paragraph contains another minor chronological error. The twenty-day gale which set in on April 19 is said to have ceased before May 2. There is a considerable probability that the former date should read "the 9th of April." Printers habitually read off a fairly long phrase or sentence from a manuscript and set it from memory: if the compositor of the *Travels* worked in this manner it is easy to understand how the similarity of "9th" and "19th" could have brought about the mistake. Another possible example of this kind of slip occurs near the end of the third voyage.

The remainder of the second voyage presents no difficulties. Gulliver landed in Brobdingnag on June 17, 1703, and was taken to the farmhouse on the same day. He began his tour of the country "upon the *17th* of *August*, about two Months after [his] Arrival," (2.2.6) and reached Lorbrulgrud, after ten weeks, on October 26 (2.2.7-8). Here, after a "few Weeks" (2.3.1), he was bought by the Queen. There are no further statements about the times of Gulliver's adventures until the second paragraph of the last chapter of the voyage, where he observes, "I had now been two Years in this Country; and about the beginning of the third, *Glumdalclitch* and I attended the King and Queen in a Progress to the South Coast of the Kingdom." This progress must have taken place during the summer of 1705, and the arrival at Flanflasnic, at the end of the journey (2.8.3), presumably occurred late in the summer. This agrees exactly with the only other pertinent bit of information which Swift gives us. ". . . I never went out of the Ship," Gulliver asserts, "till we came into the Downs, which was on the 3d. Day of *June*, 1706, about nine Months after my Escape."

The chronology of the last voyage is equally simple. Once again there is a minor discrepancy between the dates and the elapsed time of Gulliver's sojourn in England between voyages. He returned from Laputa on April 10, 1710, and sailed from Portsmouth on the second of August following (3.11.7:

4.1.1) : this is a little short of four months, instead of five, as the first edition has it. Gulliver was marooned in Houyhnhnm-land on May 9, 1711 (4.1.3) : after this there are no clues to the calendar until the latter part of the book. The quadrennial assembly which decided upon the exile of Gulliver met at the vernal equinox, that is, about September 21, since the country lay south of the equator (4.8.16), and about three months before Gulliver's departure (4.9.1). This last is a loose state-ment : apparently the three months' interval occurred between the assembly and the notice to depart given to Gulliver by his master, which on this supposition should be dated December 21 or thereabouts. Gulliver was allowed two months to build a boat, but completed its construction in a little more than six weeks (4.10.9, 12). The date given for his departure, Feb-ruary 15, 1715 (4.11.1) is consequently in strict accord with his other statements.

Two passages elsewhere in the text have led to some mis-understanding. Gulliver begins the fourth paragraph of the eighth chapter : "Having lived three Years in this Country, the Reader I suppose will expect that I should, like other Travellers, give him some Account of the Manners and Customs of its Inhabitants. . . ." In the seventh paragraph of the twelfth chapter, recounting his capture by the Portuguese sailors, Gulliver says, "I told them, I was born in *England*, from whence I came about five Years ago. . . ." There is no discrepancy between these two statements. Gulliver was speak-ing in round numbers. His voyage had lasted more than nine months before he was marooned. He dwelt with the Houyhn-hnms precisely three years, nine months, and six days ; when he was picked up by the Portuguese, on February 20, 1715, he had been absent from England exactly four years, six months, and eighteen days—a little nearer five years than four. The editor of the edition of 1735, not remembering these facts, emended a passage a little later on (4.11.10), in which Gul-liver spoke of his three years' residence in Houyhnhnmland, to read "five years' residence." This mistake persists in many modern editions.

The time-scheme of the first voyage falls into two parts,

each detailed and coherent in itself, and not inconsistent with
the other. Gulliver sailed from Bristol on May 4, 1699 (1.1.4),
and on the return from a prosperous voyage to the Pacific
Ocean his ship foundered off the coast of Lilliput on November 5. The year is not stated, but subsequent events show that
it was 1700. On the morning after the wreck Gulliver found
himself in captivity, and on the next day he arrived at Mil-
dendo. About three weeks later (November 28, approximately) he had learned the language of Lilliput sufficiently
well to permit him to converse with the Emperor (1.2.6), and
to be partially intelligible to the officers who searched his
pockets. Their inventory is dated "the fourth Day of the
eighty ninth Moon" of the Emperor's reign (1.2.9). The
articles by the terms of which Gulliver gained his freedom are
dated "the twelfth Day of the Ninety-first moon" (1.3.18).
"Moon," presumably, means a lunar month of twenty-eight
days, in which case the date of Gulliver's release came at the
end of January or the beginning of February, 1701. "About
a Fortnight" later Reldresal made a visit to Gulliver to ac-
quaint him with the political state of the kingdom (1.4.4).
Here, in the middle of February, the first series of dates comes
to an end: there is no clear indication of the length of time
spent by Gulliver in maturing his plan for the attack on
Blefuscu and carrying it into effect. A second series of dates
begins, however, with Gulliver's capture of the Blefuscudian
fleet. The plot against Gulliver broke out "less than two
Months" after he had refused to help enslave Blefuscu, which
he seems to have done immediately after his great exploit
(1.5.4, 5). The ambassadors from Blefuscu arrived in Lilliput "about three Weeks" after their naval disaster (1.5.6),
but this period seems to have been overlapped by the two-
month interval just referred to, and if this is true it may be
ignored in the chronology. A "considerable Person at Court"
warned Gulliver of the plot just before it was to have been put
into execution, and in consequence Gulliver fled to Blefuscu
three days later. The exact date of this flight is fixed by the
statement (1.6.19) that Gulliver resided in Lilliput for nine
months and thirteen days: he departed, therefore, on August

18, 1701. Reckoning backward about two months (the duration of the plot) gives the middle of June as the time of the falling-out of Gulliver and the Emperor. By this calculation the whole affair of the fleet occupied about four months: but this period may have been shorter if it took Gulliver some time to persuade the Emperor to order the inventory, in which case the dates immediately preceding the naval victory should be set somewhat later.

The remainder of the calendar is straightforward. Gulliver discovered a derelict boat on August 21, three days after his arrival in Blefuscu (1.8.1): he spent ten days in making paddles, and brought the boat into the royal port for repairs (1.8.2). He finished these in "about a Month" (1.8.7), and set sail on September 24, 1701 (1.8.9). Two days later he was picked up by an English vessel, which eventually landed him in the Downs on April 13, 1702.

The chronology of the third voyage is by far the most complex and unsatisfactory. The *Hope-well* sailed from England on August 6, 1706, and is said to have reached Fort St. George (Madras) on April 11, 1707: here the ship stayed for three weeks, and then spent an unspecified time in sailing to Tongking (3.1.3). Shortly after the arrival in that port Gulliver set out in a sloop, and eighteen days later he was captured by pirates (3.1.4), who set him adrift. Five days later still he was found by the Laputans and taken up into their flying island (3.1.8-10). He learned the language in "about a Months time" (3.2.18), and spent two months there all told (3.4.2). As the date of his departure is given specifically as February 16 (3.4.6), it is possible by reckoning backward two months and twenty-three days to set November 24 as the approximate time of departure from Tongking. Working still farther backward, we find that the voyage from Madras to Tongking occupied the period from the beginning of May to the middle of November: this is perhaps a little long, but not at all implausible. Going forward from February 16 again, Gulliver spent "a few days" with Lord Munodi (3.4.16), and one or two more in the Grand Academy of Lagado. Perhaps a week more was spent in the overland journey of a hundred and forty miles to the port of Maldonada (3.7.1). Gulliver then spent ten days on the island of Glubbdubdrib (3.7.6), and another fortnight in Maldonada waiting for his ship, which carried him to Luggnagg in a month. This all adds up to something over two months, which agrees with the date given for the arrival in Luggnagg—April 21 (3.9.1).

At this point difficulties begin. The year should be 1708, but in the first edition it is 1711, which is clearly wrong. The edition of 1735 made the apparently obvious correction to 1708, ignoring the fact that Gulliver, after what is clearly a short stay in Luggnagg (he had not even time to learn the language), departed for Japan in 1709. One easy way out of the maze is to substitute 1708 for 1707 as the year of the arrival in Madras and 1709 for 1711 as that of the landing in Luggnagg. But this gives an abnormally long voyage from England to Madras,[12] and adding a year to the time spent between Madras and Tongking is equally unsatisfactory. For the moment it will be well to adopt 1709 as the year of arrival in Luggnagg and take a fresh start.

The sojourn in Luggnagg, brief as it is, produces its own crux. Gulliver landed on April 21, and left on May 6, 1709 (3.11.4). In the meantime, however, he observes (3.9.7), "I stayed three Months in this Country. . . ." This statement, which is in a passage not primarily concerned with the chronology, and which is some distance from other statements of that kind, may be due to an oversight in revision: there is no possible way of harmonizing it with the text.

Three weeks after Gulliver's departure from Luggnagg he landed in Japan at the mouth of Tokio Bay (3.11.4). He was immediately sent to Yedo (Tokio), about forty miles away, and his audience with the Emperor probably took place on the following day, May 28. He was then convoyed south by a body of troops on the march to Nangasac (Nagasaki), in which city he arrived on June 9, 1709, "after a very long and troublesome Journey." The distance, by Moll's map, is over five hundred miles: in actual fact it is a good deal greater. The average daily distance traveled would therefore have been more than forty miles—a practical impossibility if much of the trip was made overland. But as Yedo and Nagasaki are on different islands, some of the traveling, and perhaps most of it, must have been by sea.

From Nagasaki Gulliver sailed to Amsterdam in the *Amboyna*, and thence to England in a small vessel. According to the first edition, the landing in Amsterdam took place on April 16, 1710, and the arrival in England on April 10 (3.11.6, 7). Some editors have assumed a simple transposition of these dates by the printer: others have preferred to change the second date to April 20. It seems more likely that this is another instance of a compositor's error like that conjectured at the beginning of the second voyage: if so, the true date of the debarkation at Amsterdam was April 6, and the similarity between "sixth" and "sixteenth" led to the confusion in the mind of the typesetter.

The final difficulty with the chronology of this voyage is found in the last paragraph, which stated, in the first edition, that Gulliver's absence from England had been for "Five Years and Six Months compleat." The elapsed time from August 5, 1706, to April 10, 1710, is a little over three years and eight months. The mistake suggests one possible reason which may underlie all the chronological discrepancies of the voyage. It is worth remarking that the other serious errors occur in the ninth and tenth chapters, which are concerned with Luggnagg. If in the original draft the voyage had been intended to occupy over five years, and especially if a visit to another country had intervened between the stay in Balnibarbi and the visit to Luggnagg, then the date "1711" (3.9.1) and the other and lesser discrepancies in these chapters are easily explained as oversights in revision. The explanation is tempting, but it must be admitted that there is no external evidence to support it.

Only one statement remains to be discussed. "Thus, Gentle Reader," says Gulliver at the beginning of the twelfth chapter of the last voyage, "I have given thee a faithful History of my Travels for Sixteen Years, and above Seven Months." Here, at least, Swift was on his guard: the voyage to Lilliput began on May 4, 1699; the final return to England took place

on December 5, 1715. This accuracy is more characteristic of
Swift's dealing with time in the *Travels* than is the carelessness which is evident in a few places at the end of the third
voyage. One possible explanation of the major discrepancies
has already been proposed, but of course any or all of these, as
well as the trifling mistakes, may have been due to copyists or
typesetters. Swift's complaints in the *Letter to Sympson* have
a ring of sincerity: "I find likewise, that your Printer hath
been so careless as to confound the Times, and mistake the
Dates of my several Voyages and Returns; neither assigning
the true Year, or the true Month, or Day of the Month: and
I hear the original Manuscript is all destroyed, since the Publication of my Book." (Par. 4.) The natural question, of
course, is: If this was the case, why did not Ford include the
correct dates in his list of emendations, or in his corrected
copy of the first edition? To this there can be no positive
answer: the most probable is that the errors had already crept
into the manuscript, which Ford followed mechanically in his
collation, not concerning himself even with the most glaring
chronological inconsistencies. There is at least some evidence
for this in the fact that he passed over the date "1711," in
3.9.1, and the obvious contradiction of dates at the end of the
third voyage which brought Gulliver home six days before his
intermediate sojourn in Amsterdam.

Personal and Political Satire in Gulliver's Travels

NO one who reads a modern annotated edition of *Gulliver's Travels* can fail to observe the abundance of the commentary upon the first and third voyages and the comparative scarcity of it in connection with the second and fourth. The reason for this, of course, is that the first and third voyages are primarily satiric in tone, with frequent references to contemporary persons and events in western Europe. On the other hand, since Brobdingnag and Houyhnhnmland are in differing degrees Utopian commonwealths, Swift has no desire to identify their ruling classes with those of his own country. There are a few scattered exceptions which are worth remark. The maids of honor at the court of George I regarded the account of their Brobdingnagian counterparts (2.5.6, 7) as a direct insult.[1] King George himself is ridiculed as a foreigner in a not too cautious passage in the second chapter of the same voyage (2.2.2), and again in the fourth voyage as one of the beggarly German princes who hire out troops (4.5.5). And in the descriptions of Europe which Gulliver gives to the King of Brobdingnag and to his master Houyhnhnm there are, in the midst of much general satire, a few attacks on identifiable individuals.

Most of these references, however, seem to be incidental and opportunistic. It is not strange, perhaps, that the personal attacks in the two primarily satiric voyages have generally been held to be equally planless—a sort of literary Donnybrook Fair, in which Swift followed the good old Irish maxim, "Whenever you see a head, hit it!" Consequently no one has been greatly disturbed by allegorical interpretations of the first voyage which identify Gulliver now as Oxford, now as

Bolingbroke, and now as Swift himself. As the careers of both of the first two politicians undoubtedly contribute incidents to Gulliver's career, the burden of proof lies on the shoulders of anyone who argues that the political allegory is consistent.

Consistency can be obtained, however, by supposing that Gulliver's career in Lilliput represents the joint political fortunes of Oxford and Bolingbroke during the latter half of Queen Anne's reign, when the two men shared the leadership of the Tory party. This device permits Swift to make use of the most dramatic incidents from the life of each man, and at the same time to avoid too close a parallel with the life of either.

The allegory is exactly coincidental with Gulliver's residence in Lilliput and Blefuscu. It begins with the hero's shipwreck and captivity, which correspond to the temporary fall from power of Oxford and Bolingbroke (then Robert Harley and Henry St. John) in 1708, when the Whigs, led by Godolphin and Marlborough, secured control of the Cabinet and the House of Commons. These events take place in the first chapter of the voyage, in which the nature of the allegory is not yet so clearly apparent. Looking back from later chapters, however, it is possible to extract a number of probable allusions to events of the years 1708-1710. Gulliver is pictured as having been caught off guard; as contemplating violence against his enemies, then as deciding upon submission as the more prudent course, and later as regarding this submission as a tacit promise binding him in honor not to injure his captors even when it lies within his power to do so. It is hardly necessary to point out the parallel between this conduct and that of the Tory leaders toward the Whigs.

In the second chapter we are introduced to the Emperor and to another simplification of history. Swift is telling a story which began in the reign of Anne and ended in that of George I. To supply Lilliput with an Empress and an Emperor reigning successively would have been to make the author's meaning dangerously plain: it was safer to make them husband and wife. For the same reason the Emperor was described as being almost the exact antithesis of George:

> He is taller by almost the breadth of my Nail, than any of his Court, which alone is enough to strike an Awe into the Beholders. His Features are strong and masculine, with an *Austrian* Lip and arched Nose, his Complexion olive, his Countenance erect, his Body and Limbs well proportioned, all his Motions graceful, and his Deportment majestick. He was then past his Prime, being twenty-eight Years and three Quarters old, of which he had reigned about seven, in great Felicity, and generally victorious. . . . His Dress was very plain and simple, and the Fashion of it between the *Asiatic* and the *European*; but he had on his Head a light Helmet of Gold, adorned with Jewels, and a Plume on the Crest. He held his Sword drawn in his Hand, to defend himself, if I should happen to break loose; it was almost three Inches long, the Hilt and Scabbard were Gold enriched with Diamonds. His Voice was shrill, but very clear and articulate, and I could distinctly hear it when I stood up. (1.2.3.)

When one recalls George's thick and ungainly form, his bad taste in dress, and his guttural and unintelligible pronunciation of the little English he knew, it becomes clear that Swift is employing with unusual effectiveness the same technique that Pope was to use a few years later when he caricatured George II in the *Epistle to Augustus*. "Praise undeserved is scandal in disguise."

The most important event in the second chapter is the making of the inventory of Gulliver's possessions by a committee appointed by the Emperor. This, probably, stands for the investigation, by a committee of Whig lords, of one William Gregg, a clerk in Harley's office who had been guilty of treasonable correspondence with France. No evidence was found to implicate Harley in the affair, and he, of course, strenuously protested his innocence and his loyalty. This is reflected in a sentence describing what took place at the reading of the inventory. "In the mean time [the Emperor] ordered three thousand of his choicest Troops (who then attended him) to surround me at a distance, with their Bows and Arrows just ready to discharge: but I did not observe it, for my Eyes were wholly fixed upon his Majesty." (1.2.10.)

With the third chapter events begin to move more rapidly. Gulliver's gentleness and good behavior impress the Emperor and the populace favorably, and he becomes more and more importunate for his release. This is opposed only by Skyresh Bolgolam, a cabinet minister who, when finally overborne by the other authorities, manages at least to provide that Gulliver's liberty shall be hedged about with restrictions. This corresponds to a series of political developments which culminated early in 1711. The Tories gradually won their way back into public favor: the Queen had always been inclined toward them. The identity of Skyresh Bolgolam has been a matter of dispute. William Cooke Taylor thought he might be the Duke of Argyle, whom Swift had offended by his attacks on the Scotch.[2] Sir Charles Firth pointed out that Bolgolam was described as being "of a morose and sour Complection," and proposed the name of the Earl of Nottingham, because there was mutual enmity between Swift and the Earl.[3] Swift had, indeed, been the instrument of fixing upon the Earl the sobriquet of "Dismal."[4] Both these identifications rest, however, upon the supposition that Gulliver is Swift, and both men had good reason for hating the author, whereas Gulliver protests (1.3.8) that Bolgolam's hatred arose "without any provocation." Now Nottingham was also an enemy of Harley, on no better ground than that the latter had succeeded him in office in 1704. Moreover, while the Earl never proposed anything resembling a set of conditions on which Swift might be allowed liberty, he did, in 1711, execute a political maneuver which could easily have been interpreted in these terms with regard to Harley. On the latter's rise to power as Chancellor of the Exchequer (in effect Prime Minister) Nottingham proposed in the House of Lords an amendment to the royal address which stipulated that no peace with France should be made which left Spain and the Indies in the possession of the House of Bourbon.[5] This was an open attempt to restrict the powers of the new Tory administration, and to embarrass them by the implication that they could not be trusted to safeguard the interests of England. Harley and St. John felt it prudent not to oppose this amendment, and it was consequently carried. This is expressed allegorically by Gulliver's remark, "I swore and subscribed to these Articles with great Chearfulness and Content, although some of them were not so honourable as I could have wished; which proceeded wholly from the Malice of *Skyresh Bolgolam* the High Admiral: ..." (1.3.19.)[6]

The articles to which Gulliver swore are not all of the same kind. Most of them are amusing provisions arising out of the difference in size between him and the Lilliputians. But two are connected with the underlying narrative. The first provides that Gulliver shall not leave Lilliput without the Emperor's license given under the great seal. The sixth requires Gulliver to be the Emperor's ally against Blefuscu, and to do his utmost to destroy the enemy's fleet. The true significance of these stipulations does not appear until much later.

The fourth chapter is explanatory and preparatory. Swift takes an opportunity, in describing Gulliver's visit to the palace, to emphasize the Queen's complaisance toward Gulliver, or, in other words, Queen Anne's inclination toward the Tories. The chief interest of the chapter, however, lies in the detailed account of the political situation in Lilliput and the events which led up to it. There is no special significance in the fact that the narrator is Reldresal, whose identity and relationship to the allegory do not become clear until the seventh chapter. He first explains the party system, admitting that the High-Heels (Tories) exceed in number his own party, the Low-Heels (Whigs), though the latter, through the Emperor's favor, are in power: he also admits a fear that the heir to the crown (the Prince of Wales, later George II) is partial to the High-Heels, though he tries to retain the friendship of both sides. Reldresal also expounds the religious differences of the day under the guise of the dispute between the Big-Endians and the Small-Endians (Roman Catholics and Protestants). The trouble began, he relates, with the reigning Emperor's great-grandfather, who, when his son was a boy, published an edict commanding his subjects to break their eggs at the smaller end because his son had cut his fingers in breaking an egg at the larger end, according to primitive custom. The great-grandfather is Henry VIII; the son, presumably, Elizabeth, who was declared illegitimate by the Pope; the edict, Henry's proclamation of himself as head of the national church. The choice of the symbol of the egg may have been guided by a desire to refer to the Eucharist, the nature of which was the chief theological point at issue in the great schism. Reldresal reviews the controversy, in the course of which "one Emperor [Charles I] lost his Life, and another [James II] his Crown." This all leads naturally to an explanation of international relations with Blefuscu (France), which is represented as harboring and encouraging Big-Endian exiles who have fled thither after unsuccessful rebellions. This is as close as Swift comes to a reference to the Jacobite movement, but it was close enough to leave contemporary readers in no doubt as to his meaning. Finally, the War of the Spanish Succession is described as "a bloody War [that] hath been carryed on between the two Empires for six and thirty Moons with various Success." Swift, as a Tory, has no desire to exalt the Duke of Marlborough, or to make it appear that England, in 1711, was clearly superior to France in arms: consequently Reldresal's account ends upon this note, with the further addition that Lilliput is in imminent danger from attack by Blefuscu, and that the Emperor relies upon Gulliver (the Tory administration) to save the country.

The fifth chapter brings the crisis. For dramatic purposes Swift condenses into a short space of time happenings which historically took up more than two years. The first concern of Harley and St. John, on obtaining power, was peace with France. The war had become increasingly a Whig war, from which Marlborough gained military prestige and the commercial interests foresaw the destruction of France's international trade, to their own profit. The Tories, on the other hand, did not anticipate any advantages from a continuation of hostilities, which they believed could not be carried to the point of a decisive English victory. They could not negotiate openly with France, however, because the war was still generally popular, and the Whigs might raise the cry (as they did later) that the Tories were robbing England of the fruits of victory by granting the enemy easy terms. But secret negotiations also involved difficulties. England was bound by treaties not to make peace without the consent of her allies, and the ministry had no right, under English law, to enter into discussions of the peace terms without special royal authority granted under the great seal. Despite all this the administration did begin negotiations in secret, justifying this action on the ground that peace was necessary for the welfare of England. Eventually, in 1713, both countries signed a treaty at Utrecht, by the terms of which France gained more than the military situation warranted, but did agree, among other things, to dismantle the port of Dunkirk, one of the chief threats to English naval supremacy.

Swift's symbolical representation of these events is masterly. He avoids any celebration of Marlborough's military genius by making the victory over Blefuscu a naval triumph, standing for the demolition of the defenses of Dunkirk. The Whig desire for a crushing defeat of France is pictured as a malicious and despotic wish of the Emperor to humiliate and tyrannize over "a Free and Brave People." The collusion of the Tories with the French, as charged by their opponents, is explained and defended as common politeness on Gulliver's part toward the diplomatic representatives of a foreign power.

The chapter concludes with an episode which seems unconnected with what has preceded it. When one understands its real meaning, however, the chapter becomes the most completely unified in the voyage. The story of the fire in the royal palace is Swift's defense of the Tories' illegal negotiation of the peace. What Swift wanted was an instance of an emergency met by an act technically illegal, but clearly justifiable because of the dangerous circumstances. Gulliver's method of extinguishing the fire answered the purpose admirably. Critics of Swift have often complained that the allegory is needlessly gross, but this is unfair. There was more than one reason for Harley's fall from power. Almost from the time of his accession to the chancellorship he had begun to lose the personal, though not the political favor of the Queen. He had a weakness for the bottle, and pride of place combined with a contempt for Anne's intellect led him on more than one occasion to appear drunk in her presence and to use language which she felt was an affront to her dignity. Swift was aware of all this. While he was in Yorkshire in the dark days of the early summer of 1714, Erasmus Lewis had written to him from London:

> I have yours of the 25th. You judge very right; it is not the going out, but the manner, that enrages me. The Queen has told all the Lords the reasons of her parting with [Harley, now Earl of Oxford], viz. that he neglected all business; that he was seldom to be understood; that when he did explain himself, she could not depend upon the truth of what he said; that he never came to her at the time she appointed; that he often came drunk; that lastly, to crown all, he behaved himself toward her with ill manner, indecency, and disrespect. *Pudet haec opprobria nobis*, etc.[7]

The brilliance of Swift's symbolism is now clear. In a single action he embodied both the political and the personal charges against Oxford. Gulliver saved the palace, though his conduct was both illegal and indecent: Oxford saved the state, in return for which incidental illegalities and indecencies should have been overlooked. But prudery was stronger than gratitude. "I was privately assured," says Gulliver, "the Empress conceiving the greatest Abhorrence of what I had done, removed to the most distant side of the Court, firmly resolved that those Buildings should never be repaired for her Use; and in the presence of her chief Confidents, could not forbear vowing Revenge." (1.5.10.) In plain terms, Queen Anne dispensed with Oxford's services and vowed never to make use of them again.

At this point Swift, to heighten suspense, interpolates a chapter on general conditions of life in Lilliput, which, while it contains a number of isolated satiric references, does not advance the main plot. This is resumed at the beginning of the seventh chapter with the secret visit to Gulliver of "a considerable Person at Court to whom [Gulliver] had been very serviceable at a time when he lay under the highest Displeasure of his Imperial Majesty." The considerable person was no less than the Duke of Marlborough. Early in 1715 Bolingbroke heard rumors that the victorious Whigs intended to impeach him, together with Oxford and other Tory leaders, of high treason. Relying on old friendship he inquired about the truth of these rumors from Marlborough, who, seeing an opportunity to get revenge for his dismissal four years earlier, so played upon Bolingbroke's fears that he fled to France.[8] It is upon Bolingbroke's adventures that the story of Gulliver in Lilliput is based from this point onward, since Oxford, with more courage, remained to stand his trial and to be freed.

The tale of what was in store for Bolingbroke, as translated into Lilliputian terms, was sufficiently disquieting. Gulliver's enemies are listed as Skyresh Bolgolam; Flimnap, the High Treasurer; Limtoc, the General; Lalcon, the Chamberlain; and Balmuff, the Grand Treasurer. These represent Whigs or independent Tories who displayed their hostility to the Oxford-Bolingbroke administration either by speaking against it in Parliament or by acting as members of the Committee of Secrecy which, early in 1715, investigated the conduct of the ministry in the negotiation of the peace. Bolgolam has already been identified as the Earl of Nottingham, whose hatred of Oxford has been explained. Flimnap was Robert Walpole, the rising leader of the Whigs and chairman of the Committee of Secrecy. Limtoc the General, Lalcon the Chamberlain, and Balmuff the Grand Justiciary were, respectively, General Stanhope, Secretary of State for War; the Duke of Devonshire, Lord Steward; and Lord Cowper, Lord Chancellor. The second of these identifications is a little doubtful because there was in the British cabinet an official entitled Lord Chamberlain, but in 1715 this minister was the Duke of Shrewsbury, a mild man who took no active part in the attack on the defeated ministry.

All of the four articles of impeachment are counterparts of actual charges made against Oxford and Bolingbroke.[9] The first accuses Gulliver of illegally extinguishing the fire in the palace (the ministry's technically unlawful negotiation of the Peace of Utrecht). The second dwells on Gulliver's refusal to subjugate Blefuscu completely (the granting of easy terms of peace to France). The third attacks the friendliness of Gulliver and the Blefuscudian ambassadors (the secret understanding between the Tory administration and the French diplomats). The fourth asserts that Gulliver intends to visit Blefuscu with only verbal license from the Emperor (a repetition of the first charge, with special reference to the failure of Oxford to procure a license under the great seal to negotiate the peace). The second and fourth articles contain allusions to the sixth and first provisions, respectively, of the agreement by which Gulliver was set at liberty.

The report of the council at which Gulliver's fate was debated is mordantly ironic. His bitterest enemies demand that he be put to a painful and ignominious death. The Emperor is more merciful, remembering Gulliver's former services: and Reldresal, Principal Secretary of State for Private Affairs and Gulliver's "true Friend," proposes and eventually carries a more "lenient" motion. Gulliver is merely to be blinded, after which, if the council finds it expedient, he may easily be starved to death. Blinding is the equivalent of barring Oxford and Bolingbroke from political activity for the remainder of their lives. Reldresal's pretended friendship is a reference to the behavior of Charles, Viscount Townshend, Secretary of State in the Whig cabinet, whom the Tory leaders at first regarded as a friend at court after their fall, but whose sincerity they came to distrust. The "mercy" of the Emperor is a fling at the execution of a number of the leaders of the rebellion of 1715 shortly after the House of Lords, in an address to George I, had praised his "endearing tenderness and clemency." Gulliver's reaction to this clemency is illuminating in its indication of the attitude of Oxford and Bolingbroke toward the Hanoverian dynasty as Swift wished it to be understood:

> And as to myself, I must confess, having never been designed for a Courtier either by my Birth or Education, I was so ill a Judge of Things, that I could not discover the Lenity and Favour of this Sentence, but conceived it (perhaps erro-

neously) rather to be rigorous than gentle. I sometimes thought of standing my Tryal, for although I could not deny the Facts alledged in the several Articles, yet I hoped they would admit of some Extenuations. But having in my Life perused many State-Tryals, which I ever observed to terminate as the Judges thought fit to direct, I durst not rely on so dangerous a Decision, in so critical a Juncture, and against such powerful Enemies. Once I was strongly bent upon Resistance, for while I had Liberty, the whole Strength of that Empire could hardly subdue me, and I might easily with Stones pelt the Metropolis to pieces; but I soon rejected that Project with Horror, by remembering the Oath I had made to the Emperor, the Favours I received from him, and the high Title of *Nardac* he conferred upon me. Neither had I so soon learned the Gratitude of Courtiers, to persuade myself that his Majesty's present Severities acquitted me of all past Obligations. (1.7.23.)

Little more of the allegory remains to be unraveled. Gulliver prudently and secretly seeks the protection of the Emperor of Blefuscu, as Bolingbroke fled to France. Like Bolingbroke, too, Gulliver ignores a proclamation threatening to stigmatize him as a traitor unless he returns to stand trial for his alleged crimes. Here Swift breaks off: it would hardly have been politic to discuss the period during which Bolingbroke was openly Secretary of State to the Pretender. The account of Gulliver's return to Europe is, like that of his arrival in Lilliput, a narrative to be taken at its face value.

The strongest arguments in favor of this interpretation of the *Voyage to Lilliput* are its consistency and the exactness with which it follows the chronology of the events which it symbolizes. Single incidents are often open to more than one explanation: a series carries conviction in proportion to its length. There are, of course, a few cases in which Swift takes slight and unimportant liberties with chronology for the sake of simplicity. For example, he represents Gulliver as being ennobled after the capture of the fleet, whereas Oxford and Bolingbroke received their titles not after the signing of the Peace of Utrecht, but while it was still being secretly negotiated. Similarly Flimnap is represented from the beginning of the story as Prime Minister and Gulliver's most potent enemy, though Walpole did not become head of the government until 1720. Swift is careful, however, not to attribute to Walpole any act of hostility to the Tory administration for which he was not responsible.

Swift also introduces incidental satiric touches as opportunity offers wherever the events or conditions have no temporal connection with the main plot. This is especially true in the sixth chapter where, among other things, there are references to the trial of Bishop Atterbury in 1722 and 1723 (in the use of the informers Clustril and Drunlo by Flimnap, standing for Walpole's employment of the spies Pancier and Neynoe),[10] and a gratuitous gibe, in the final paragraph, at the notorious infidelities of Walpole's wife.

The political allegory of the first voyage is primarily concerned with the defense of the conduct of the Oxford-Bolingbroke ministry, and incidentally with an attack upon the Whigs. In the third voyage the emphasis is exactly reversed. It is important to realize from the beginning that the chief purpose of the allegory is *not*, as has so often been asserted, to attack the new science, but to attack learned folly, or "pedantry," to use the word in its eighteenth-century meaning, and especially innovations and innovators in general. The focus of this attack is the Whig ministry under George I, which is accused of experimentation in the field of government, and of fostering experimenters in many other fields. Whiggery, to Swift, is the negation of that certainty which results from adherence to tried and approved procedures. In the light of this interpretation of Swift's design it becomes evident that the third voyage is much more unified in purpose than has commonly been supposed. A very large preponderance of its specific references to contemporary persons and events is contained in the first four chapters. The key to the satire is the identification of Laputa, the flying island, which has been variously interpreted as the English court under George I, and as the whole of England. The former interpretation was the normal one until about half a century ago. Swift's own verse (in his poem *The Life and Character of Dr. Swift*) lends authority to this earlier view, for the supposed detractor

of the Dean who there catalogues Swift's writings lists among
them

> . . . *Libels* yet conceal'd from sight,
> Against the *Court* to show his *Spight*.
> Perhaps his *Travels, Part the Third* ;
> A *Lye* at every *second* word ;
> Offensive to a *Loyal* Ear—: . . .[11]

In 1896, however, G. A. Aitken published in an appendix
to an edition of *Gulliver's Travels* four previously unprinted
paragraphs contained in the manuscript emendations in the
Ford copy of the first edition.[12] Three years later these paragraphs, which described the rebellion of Lindalino against
Laputa, were restored to their proper place in the third chapter
of the third voyage by G. R. Dennis, who edited the *Travels*
for the Temple Scott edition.[13] The effect of the new passage
on the interpretation of the voyage was remarkable. There
could be little doubt that it was an allegorical description of
the controversy over Wood's halfpence, with which Swift had
dealt so brilliantly in the *Drapier's Letters* only two years
before *Gulliver's Travels* was published. And since Lindalino
obviously stood for Dublin, it is hardly surprising that Laputa
should have been taken for England as a whole, hovering over
all of Ireland, or Balnibarbi. In 1919 Sir Charles Firth not
only endorsed this view, but extended it to the interpretation
of other parts of the third voyage, and even allowed it to color
his ideas of the fourth. In particular he suggested that Munodi
was Viscount Midleton, Chancellor of Ireland from 1714 to
1725, and that Balnibarbi in the impoverished state described
in the third chapter represented Ireland under English domi-
nation.[14] This theory, of course, necessitates a belief that
Swift changed the meaning of his symbols from time to time :
for example, Lagado is in Balnibarbi, but the Grand Academy
of Lagado is generally identified as the Royal Society of
London ; therefore Balnibarbi, of which Lagado is the metropolis, must sometimes stand for Ireland, and sometimes for
England or for the British Isles as a whole. Other inconsistencies involved in Sir Charles's theory suggest themselves on

further examination. From the beginning of the voyage Swift makes a good deal of the minuteness of Laputa and the relatively great extent of the land of Balnibarbi which it dominates. Moreover, Laputa is inhabited only by a small number of courtiers and their hangers-on (chiefly scientific and musical); it is not self-supporting, but is dependent upon sustenance drawn from below; it travels about by a series of oblique motions which probably symbolizes the indirect and erratic course of Whig policy under the ministerial clique headed by Walpole. Lagado, the metropolis of the kingdom, which certainly stands for London, is below and subject to Laputa. Lindalino, or Dublin, is described as the second city of the kingdom—an accurate description if the kingdom is the whole British Isles, but not if it is Ireland alone. Moreover, the general account of the King's methods of suppressing insurrections which precedes the story of Lindalino's revolt is accurate only if Balnibarbi includes Great Britain.

> The King would be the most absolute Prince in the Universe, if he could but prevail on a Ministry to join with him; but these having their Estates below on the Continent, and considering that the Office of a Favourite hath a very uncertain Tenure, would never consent to the enslaving their Country. . . . nor dare his Ministers advise him to an Action, which as it would render them odious to the People, so it would be a great Damage to their own Estates, which lie all below, for the Island is the Kings Demesn. (3.3.12.)

It is hardly necessary to point out that few of George I's ministry held any significant amount of Irish land, and that none of them displayed any fear of Irish public opinion.

If the older theory, which identified Balnibarbi as England and Laputa as the Court, is reconsidered, it will be seen that one slight emendation will bring it into conformity with the account of the revolt of Lindalino. If the continent of Balnibarbi represents all of the British Isles, the inconsistencies in the allegory disappear. There can be no serious doubt that Swift, in this restored passage of *Gulliver's Travels*, is using the affair of Wood's halfpence again, but this time it is for a different purpose. In 1724, addressing Irishmen through the

Drapier's Letters, he was trying to arouse national feeling
and to make the issue one of Ireland against England. In
1726, in a more general work, addressed to the English more
than to any other nation, he made the issue one of tyranny
over the subject by a would-be absolute monarch. When this
is once understood it is not difficult to find plausible counterparts in history for the various details of the description of
the Laputian method of suppressing insurrections.

The three ways of punishing a recalcitrant city (interpos-
ing the island between the city and the sun; pelting the city
with rocks; and completely crushing it by dropping the
island down upon it) represent three degrees of severity in
actual practice, perhaps threats, accompanied by withdrawal
of court patronage; moderate civil repressive action; and military invasion. The reason given for the King's disinclination
to proceed to the last degree of severity is that this might
endanger the adamantine bottom of the island, which appears
to stand either for the monarchy or for the British constitu-
tion. It should be remembered that Swift believed in the
theory of government which divided the power among the
three estates of the realm, and which relied on a balance among
them. Any estate which arrogated to itself an undue share of
power was held to endanger the whole structure of the government.

The chief defenses of any city against oppression by the
King and his court are thus expressed allegorically:

> . . . if the Town intended to be destroyed should have in it
> any tall Rocks, as it generally falls out in the larger Cities, a
> Scituation probably chosen at first with a View to prevent such
> a Catastrophe; or if it abound in high Spires or Pillars of
> Stone, a sudden Fall might endanger the Bottom or under
> Surface of the Island. . . . (3.3.13)

Of the three defenses, the "high Spires" seem least ambigu-
ous: almost certainly these represent churches or churchmen
—possibly the ecclesiastical interest generally, which rallied
almost unanimously to the Irish cause. The "tall Rocks" seem
to differ from the "pillars of stone" chiefly in being natural
rather than creations of man, which suggests that the rocks

may represent either the hereditary nobility, who constituted the second estate of the realm, or the higher ecclesiastical authorities, representing a divine rather than a man-made institution. Similarly the "Pillars of Stone" may be either self-made citizens of power and importance, or certain man-made legal institutions. In the story of the revolt of Lindalino the strong pointed rock in the middle of the city is almost certainly the combined power of the Irish Church, centered in St. Patrick's Cathedral; and the "four large Towers" presumably stand for the four most important local governmental agencies of Ireland—the Privy Council, the Grand Jury, and the two houses of the Irish Parliament. The "vast Quantity of the most combustible Fewel" collected by the inhabitants probably stands for the multitude of incendiary pamphlets written against Wood's halfpence by Swift and others. Finally, the unsuccessful experiment made by one of the King's officers, who let down a piece of adamant from Laputa and found it so strongly drawn toward the towers and the rock that he could hardly draw it back, presumably represents the bold resistance of the Irish civil and ecclesiastical institutions to the King's measures.

That this incident could have been omitted from the text of *Gulliver's Travels* without causing an apparent break in the continuity of the story is characteristic of the structure of the third voyage, which differs markedly from that of the first. In his account of Lilliput Swift provided a climactic plot, based upon the fortunes of a particular Tory administration. In the third voyage no such plot is practicable: the history of Walpole's administration had not reached a climax in 1726, and Swift would not have wished to tell a story which could only have emphasized the success of his enemies. He therefore chose to attack the Whigs not by dramatic narrative, but by satiric portraiture. There is, consequently, no chronological scheme for the third voyage, which is a picture of conditions rather than of acts.

As in the first voyage, Swift is chary of drawing too obvious a portrait of George I. Not much is said of the physical appearance of the King of Laputa; there are, however, several references which intelligent contemporaries must have interpreted without difficulty. One is the parenthetical remark (3.2.3) about the King's "being distinguished above all his Predecessors for his Hospitality to Strangers"—a palpable hit at George's extensive appointments of Hanoverians to posts of profit in England. The last paragraph of the third chapter is still more open satire—almost dangerously open. "By a fundamental Law of this Realm," Gulliver observes, "neither the King nor either of his two elder Sons are permitted to leave the Island, nor the Queen till she is past Childbearing." No Englishman could have failed to be reminded by this sentence that the Act of Settlement had originally forbidden the departure of the sovereign from England without the express consent of Parliament, and that George I, whose journeys to his beloved Hanover aroused the general resentment of his English subjects, had persuaded Parliament to repeal this provision of the Act in 1716. George's delight in music is parodied by the description of the Laputian King's fondness for the art. Here, however, and even more in the case of the King's supposed personal interest in science, Swift modifies the actual facts for the sake of his thesis. Under the reign of Anne men of letters had received a considerable amount of royal patronage, especially during the administration of Oxford. Under the reign of George I it seemed, especially to Tory wits who had been deprived of their posts of profit, that the pendulum had swung away from the profession of literature in the direction of musicians and experimental scientists. Patronage being, at least in theory, a personal prerogative of the King, Swift in his allegory attributed the shift in patronage to the King's inclinations. How far this shift was a fact, and, if a fact, how far it was due to conscious intention on the part of the government, are matters of secondary importance to the present inquiry. It may be said, however, that while Whig writers received some government patronage during the administration of Oxford (largely because of Swift's insistence), Tory writers got very little after the Whigs came into power in 1714. Moreover, a great wave of invention and commercial exploitation of inventions coincided with the opening years of George I's reign, and scientists, notably the astronomers Newton and Flamsteed, were given generous encouragement.

The Prince of Wales, whom Swift had once portrayed as the heir to the Lilliputian crown, with one high and one low heel, is in the third voyage aligned more definitely and sympathetically with the Tories. He is described as "a great Lord at Court, nearly related to the King, and for that reason alone used with Respect." (3.4.4.) The hostility between the Prince and his father, and his consequent unpopularity in the King's court, were, of course, common knowledge. Swift represents the Prince as one who "had great natural and acquired Parts, adorned with Integrity and Honour, but so ill an Ear for Musick, that his Detractors reported he had been often known to beat Time in the wrong Place; neither could his Tutors without extreme difficulty teach him to demonstrate the most easy Proposition in the Mathematicks." (3.4.4.) It is undoubtedly true that Prince George had a supreme contempt for academic learning, and while he probably had a better knowledge of music than Swift ascribes to him here, his interest in the art fell far below his father's: his patronage of Buononcini seems to have been motivated by a desire to annoy George I by support of a supposed rival to Handel, whom the King delighted to honor.

The Prince of Laputa is not only uninterested in the subjects which engross the attention of his father's court: he is positively interested in all the other things which they neglect. Here again Swift contrasts the theoretical Whig King with the practical Tory Prince. Alone among the Laputians the latter is anxious to learn from Gulliver the laws and customs of other countries. Alone among Laputians of rank he dispenses with the services of a flapper. He makes "very wise observations" on everything Gulliver tells him, and is loath to allow the traveler to depart, although helpful and generous when Gulliver persists in his intention. Swift makes clear the Tory hopes of the early 1720's—that Prince George on his accession to the throne might call the old Tory administration to power—through the Laputian Prince's recommendation of

Gulliver to a friend of his in Lagado, the lord Munodi, who has been variously identified with Bolingbroke[15] and Lord Midleton,[16] but never, apparently, with Oxford, whom he actually represents. The evidence for this identification is plentiful. Munodi is described as a former governor of Lagado, which must be translated either as Lord Mayor of London or Prime Minister of England. As Swift displays no interest in the municipal government of London, the second alternative is much more probable. Munodi is represented as having been discharged from office for inefficiency by a cabal of ministers—a close parallel with Oxford's dismissal from his post in 1714 and his trial on the charge of treason between 1715 and 1717. It will be recalled that when the accusation against Oxford was finally dropped in 1717 he returned from politics to the quiet existence of a country gentleman on his estates in Herefordshire. This retirement is reflected not only in Munodi's having withdrawn from public life, but in his name, which seems to be a contraction of *"mundum odi"*—"I hate the world."

Munodi's story is a thinly veiled allegory of the results to be expected from flighty experimental Whig government as opposed to sound conservative Tory government. Balnibarbi, the inhabitants of which are occupied with financial speculation and with the exploitation of chimerical "projects," both in the city and in the country, is a symbol of the British Isles under George I and the Whigs: Munodi's private estate, managed in "the good old way," to the evident profit of its owner and the pleasure of its citizenry, represents the way of life of the Tory remnant, sneered at by the adherents of the newer way as reactionary. The triumph of the innovators is attributed to the conversion of weak-minded members of the governing class by the court circle in Laputa, with the result that their principles have been imported into the management of the subject continent, and a center of the new experimental culture has even been founded in Lagado. The Grand Academy no doubt stands in part for the Royal Society, and the fact that Swift in his allegory lays its creation at the door of the court is significant as indicating the center of his interest, since the Royal Society, while it had received encouragement from the court of Charles II at the time of its foundation in 1660, certainly had more influence on the court of George I than the court had upon it.

The last detail in the history of Munodi is of particular interest, since its true significance seems never to have been pointed out by any commentator upon the *Travels*, though it must have been apparent to many of Swift's contemporaries. There was one act of Oxford's administration which laid him open to criticism as an experimenter in governmental economics—an experimenter more speculative and unsound than any Whig. The act was the sponsoring of the South Sea Company. This device for refunding the public debt of England had been urged upon Oxford by Defoe, who had finally persuaded his superior to give the company a charter in 1712, and to arrange for the exchange of governmental obligations for South Sea stock. The public was encouraged to make the exchange on the ground that the new investment was quite as safe as the old and much more profitable. The details of the great speculation and of the ultimate crash of 1720—the "South Sea year"— need not be rehearsed in detail. The crash brought with it much criticism of Oxford, and many demands that he emerge from retirement to assist in clearing up the mess for which he was responsible. Swift does what he can to rehabilitate Oxford's reputation as an economist through the allegory of the mill, near the end of the fourth chapter. Gulliver relates that there had been on Munodi's estate (England under Oxford's administration) an old mill (the old English fiscal system), turned by the current of a large river (England's income from agriculture and trade), and sufficient not only for Munodi's family (the British empire), but also for a great number of his tenants (England's allies in the War of the Spanish Succession). A club of projectors (Defoe and his abettors) proposed to destroy the old mill and substitute a new one much farther away (the South Sea Company), requiring artificial means (stockjobbing) to pump up water for its operation the plea that water agitated by wind and air upon a he (money put into active circulation by speculation) would th the mill with half the current of a river whose course was more upon the level (would provide sufficient government revenues with the use of half the capital required by the old fiscal policy). Munodi, "being then not very well with the Court" (Anne had shown her displeasure at Oxford's personal behavior toward her as early as 1712), and being pressed by many of his friends, complied with the proposal. It is hardly necessary to labor the significance of the rest of the allegory. "After employing an Hundred Men for two Years, the Work miscarryed, the Projectors went off, laying the blame entirely upon him, railing at him ever since, and putting others upon the same Experiment, with equal Assurance of Success, as well as equal Disappointment."

The fifth and sixth chapters of the third voyage are concerned with the Grand Academy of Lagado, generally held to stand for the Royal Society of London. That the Society was in Swift's mind cannot be doubted, but that it is the primary object of the satire in these chapters is a conclusion that deserves examination, at least. The first discrepancy in the account has to do with the physical appearance of the Academy's buildings. "This Academy," says Gulliver, "is not an entire single Building, but a Continuation of several Houses on both sides of a Street; which growing wast, was purchased and applyed to that Use." (3.5.1.) The description does not fit the buildings of the real Society, which in 1710 had moved its Museum from Arundel House to a building in Crane Court, Fleet Street, quite unlike the structure pictured by Gulliver. In the light of the emphasis placed on the Academy's school of political projectors it is not impossible that the description should be applied rather to the rapidly expanding governmental buildings on both sides of Whitehall.

Far more interesting than the outward appearance of the Academy is the nature of the activities carried on within. Many of the Royal Society's experiments were in the realm of pure science, and were conducted for no immediately practical end. In the Academy the large majority of the projects are designed to bring about supposed improvements in commerce, medicine, or some other field of importance in daily life: what is ridiculous is that the methods, rather than the purposes of the inventors, are chimerical. Another important fact is the insistence upon the word "PROJECTORS" in the title of the Academy: it is printed in capitals, and it occurs, together with the word "projects," again and again in this section of the voyage. These words were not very frequently applied to members of the Royal Society and their exercises in the seventeenth and eighteenth centuries: the usual terms of contempt were "virtuosi" and "experiments." "Projector" was, however, a word all too familiar to Englishmen of the second decade of the eighteenth century. To them it signified a man who promoted a get-rich-quick scheme, plausible but impracticable, for the carrying out of which he levied upon the public. This latter habit seems to be alluded to twice in the fifth chapter: first, when Gulliver remarks that it is customary for the projectors to beg money from all who visit them (3.5.3), and secondly, when the inventor of the frame for writing books suggests that his operations "might be still improved, and much expedited, if the Publick would raise a Fund for making and employing five hundred such Frames in *Lagado*." (3.5.16.) Speculative schemes actually floated during the first six years of the reign of George I, and especially in 1720—the "South Sea year"—were in some instances almost as illusory as those described by Swift, and may even have suggested a few of them. Companies advertising for subscriptions included one for extracting silver from lead, and others for making bays in Colchester and elsewhere, for manuring farm lands, for a more inoffensive method of emptying and cleansing "necessary houses," for bringing live sea-fish to London in specially built tank-vessels, for making salt water fresh, for planting mulberry trees and raising silkworms in Chelsea Park, for fishing for wrecks along the Irish coast, for a wheel for perpetual motion, and, finally, for "an undertaking which shall in due course be revealed." An anonymous wag advertised for subscriptions to a company for melting down sawdust and chips and casting them into clean deal boards without cracks or knots: another group, having obtained several hundred subscriptions to a scheme almost equally vague, publicly announced that the venture had been a hoax intended to make the public more cautious, and returned the subscription money.[17]

The school for political projectors clearly has no connection with the Royal Society: it is a satiric attack on corruption and stupidity in government, with a section at the end based upon what Swift regarded as the biased and unjust prosecution of Bishop Atterbury, in 1723, for complicity in the Jacobite plot. The paragraph on copromancy (3.6.10) arises from the putting in evidence at the trial of the Bishop of correspondence found in his closestool.[18] The discussion of secret codes which follows has to do with the charge that the Bishop and his correspondents used the name of the Bishop's lame dog Harlequin as a symbol for the Pretender: hence the inclusion by Swift in his burlesque secret code of "a *lame Dog,* an *Invader.*"[19] This code, incidentally, was one of the few passages which Motte altered out of an apparent fear that the satire was too obvious and too dangerous. His emendations, aside from a slight rearrangement, consisted of the omission of four code pairs and the alteration of another. The phrases omitted were: "a close-stool a privy council, a flock of geese a senate, . . . a codshead a ——, . . . a gibbet a secretary of state": the alteration consisted of the weakening of "a buzzard a prime minister" to "a *Buzzard* a *great Statesman.*" Presumably the blank after "codshead" was to be filled in by the reader with "king." It is not difficult to understand why Motte, in 1726, preferred not to print this part of the manuscript as it stood.

The last type of code discussed is the anagram, a device which was also alleged to be used by the Jacobites. Swift's Tribnian experts, analyzing the sentence, "*Our Brother Tom has just got the Piles,*" produce the message, "*Resist; a Plot is brought Home, The Tour.*" It is not an accident that while the "a" in this message is a lower-case letter, the "T" of "The" is a capital. "The Tour" is a signature. During part of his exile in France Bolingbroke requested his friends to address him as M. La Tour.[20] A grammarian would point out that "la tour" is a tower: a tour is "le tour": but Swift apparently did not regard this as a serious objection. Perhaps, too, he did not wish to abandon what he felt was a very appropriate anagram.

The remainder of the third voyage contains only scattering references to specific events or persons contemporary with Swift. In the seventh chapter it is sufficiently clear that the "modern representative" of assemblies, which compares so unfavorably with the senate of ancient Rome, is the British Parliament. In the next chapter the nameless ghost in Glubbdubdrib who informs Gulliver about the confounding of the commentators on Homer and Aristotle may be Sir William Temple, whose views on classical scholarship Swift had espoused so warmly in *The Battle of the Books*, but there is not enough evidence to confirm this surmise. In the following paragraph Aristotle decries the theory of gravitation propounded by Sir Isaac Newton, one of Swift's enemies. Shortly afterward occurs one of the most mysterious references in the entire *Travels*. In the midst of a series of general exposures of the true genealogies and histories of "great families" Gulliver observes that he learned in Glubbdubdrib "whence it came what *Polydore Virgil* says of a certain great House, '*Nec Vir fortis, nec Fœmina Casta.*'" A careful search of the works of Polydore Virgil has not brought this phrase to light: on the other hand, it is the exact converse of a much-quoted sentence, famous in that day, from the epitaph on the tomb of Margaret Cavendish, Duchess of Newcastle, born Margaret Lucas: "All the brothers were valiant, and all the sisters virtuous." (Addison quoted the phrase in *The Spectator*, June 23, 1711.) As Swift seems to have had no personal animus against the Lucases, and as that family, more than most, deserved the monumental flattery, it is possible that Swift merely borrowed and twisted an effective phrase to enforce a general satire on the nobility.

One last passage in the eighth chapter contains enough specific detail to suggest a reference to an individual. This is the paragraph which reads:

> Among the rest there was one Person whose Case appeared a little singular. He had a Youth about eighteen Years old

standing by his side. He told me he had for many Years been Commander of a Ship, and in the Sea Fight at *Actium*, had the good Fortune to break through the Enemy's great Line of Battle, sink three of their Capital Ships, and take a fourth, which was the sole Cause of *Anthony's* Flight, and of the Victory that ensued; that the Youth standing by him, his only Son, was killed in the Action. He added, that upon the Confidence of some Merit, this War being at an end, he went to *Rome*, and solicited at the Court of *Augustus* to be preferred to a greater Ship, whose Commander had been killed; but without any regard to his Pretensions, it was given to a Youth who had never seen the Sea, the son of *Libertina*, who waited on one of the Emperor's Mistresses. Returning back to his own Vessels, he was charged with neglect of Duty, and the Ship was given to a Favourite Page of *Publicola* the Vice-Admiral; whereupon he retired to a poor Farm, at a great distance from *Rome*, and there ended his Life. I was so curious to know the truth of this Story, that I desired *Agrippa* might be called, who was Admiral in that Fight. He appeared and confirmed the whole Account, but with much more Advantage to the Captain, whose Modesty had extenuated or concealed a great part of his Merit. (3.8.9.)

The general purport of the third voyage suggests that this is an allegorical account of an individual instance of Whig ingratitude toward a Tory. The two most eminent Tory "martyrs" of the day were General Webb, whose exploits had been slighted by Marlborough, and Charles Mordaunt, third Earl of Peterborough. The latter military leader, a personal friend of Swift's, had fought both on land and at sea during the War of the Spanish Succession, but after some brilliant successes in the Peninsular campaign of 1706 he disagreed with the other leaders of the Allies, and was eventually recalled to England. In 1707, on the way to Genoa, his ship was attacked by the enemy; he escaped, but a convoying ship under the command of his son was badly damaged, and the son received grave wounds which may have contributed to his death some time later.[21] Peterborough's removal from command, and his failure to secure reinstatement, were at least partly due to the enmity of the young Emperor Charles, who suc-

ceeded him in the direction of the Peninsular campaign.[22]
Swift, in *The Conduct of the Allies*, had already taken up the
cudgels for Peterborough, though without naming him ex-
plicitly:

> . . . there [in Spain] we drove on the war at a prodigious
> disadvantage . . . and by a most corrupt management, the only
> general who, by a course of conduct and fortune almost mirac-
> ulous, had nearly put us into possession of the kingdom, was
> left wholly unsupported, exposed to the envy of his rivals,
> disappointed by the caprices of a young unexperienced prince,
> under the guidance of a rapacious German ministry, and at
> last called home in discontent.[23]

The young unexperienced prince was, of course, the Emperor
Charles. It seems not unlikely that he was the "youth who had
never seen the sea," who displaced the Roman hero of Gulliver's tale. The identity of the "favourite page of Publicola"
does not appear.

Perhaps the most striking feature of this explanation of the
personal and political allegory is that it leaves no room for
an autobiographical interpretation of *Gulliver's Travels*. The
various passages upon which this interpretation has rested are
seen to be susceptible of other meanings more significant in
themselves, and more consistent with each other and with the
intent of the book. If this view is correct, Swift, so often conceived as the complete egoist, did not regard his own fortunes
and misfortunes as being of equal importance with the affairs
of public figures such as Oxford, Bolingbroke, and Peterborough. This is confirmed by his correspondence. Swift
evidently felt that both Whigs and Tories were ungrateful to
him, but his services to the Whigs were, as far as we know,
relatively slight. His pamphleteering for the Tories, on the
other hand, was of inestimable value, yet for years Oxford
slighted him in favor of less deserving men, and finally obtained for him a post which he regarded as little else than
exile, and which he accepted in a mood of bitterness. On April
16, 1713, he wrote to Stella,

> Mr Lewis tells me that D. Ormd has been today with
> Qu[een] & she was content that Dr Stearn should be Bp of

Dromore and I Dean of St Patricks, but then out came Ld Tr, & sd he would not be satisfied, but that I must be Prebend of Windsor, thus he perplexes things—I expect neither; but I confess, as much as I love Engld, I am so angry at this Treatmt, that if I had my Choice I would rather have St Patricks.[24]

That this was no passing mood is shown by his letter of July 13, 1714, written from Letcombe to John Arbuthnot when it was evident that the Tory ministry had run its race:

Dear ——— I wonder how you came to mention that business to Lady M[asham], if I guess right, that the business is the Histor[ian]'s Place. It is in the D[uke] of Shr[ewsbury]'s gift, and he sent L[or]d Bol[ingbroke] word that though he was under some engagement, he would give it me. Since which time I never mentioned it, though I had a memorial some months in my pocket, which I believe you saw, but I would never give it Lady M[asham] because things were embroiled with her. I would not give two pence to have it for the value of it, but I have been told by L[or]d P[eterborough] L[a]dy M[asham] and you, that the Qu[een] has a concern for her History, &c., and I was ready to undertake it. I thought L[or]d Bol[ingbroke] would have done such a trifle, but I shall not concern myself, and I should be sorry the Qu[een] should be asked for it otherwise than as what would be for her honor and reputation with posterity, etc. Pray, how long do you think I should be suffered to hold that post in the next reign? I have enclosed sent you the original memorial as I intended it; and if L[or]d Bol[ingbroke] thinks it of any moment, let him do it, but do not give him the memorial unless he be perfectly willing. For I insist again upon it, that I am not asking a favor, and there is an end of that matter, only one word more, that I would not accept it if offered, only that it would give me an opportunity of seeing those I esteem and love the little time that they will be in power. . . . I must repeat it again, that if L[or]d Bol[ingbroke] be not full as ready to give this memorial enclosed, as you are to desire him, let it drop, for in the present view of things, I am perfectly indifferent, for I think every reason for my leaving you is manifestly doubled within these 6 weeks, by your own account as well as that of others. Besides I take it perfectly ill that The Dragon,[25] who promised me so solemnly last year to make me easy in my debts, has never done the least thing to it. So that I can safely say I never received a penny from a minister in my life. And though I scorn to complain, yet to you I will speak it, that I am very uneasy in my Fortune, having received such accounts of my agent's management that I am likely to lose near 300 pounds, beside the heavy debts I lie under at a season of my life when I hoped to have no cares of that sort.[26]

In the face of this ingratitude to himself, which he so clearly recognized, Swift nevertheless remained loyal to the defeated leaders, offering to accompany Oxford into retirement, and steadfastly defending both Oxford and Bolingbroke while they lay under charges of treason, even after Bolingbroke fled to France and joined the Pretender. All this was done, as Swift's letters show, in the face of a conviction that he himself could gain nothing from his friendship save, perhaps, a reputation of being himself a Jacobite traitor. Is it too difficult to suppose that he did this because of a sincere belief that the Tories' ingratitude to him was outweighed by their devotion to what were, in Swift's mind, the right principles of government?

The Significance
of Gulliver's Travels

THE history of the composition of *Gulliver's Travels* has been in dispute since the eighteenth century. In the years immediately following the death of Swift two of his biographers, Orrery[1] and Deane Swift,[2] maintained that the book had been written in the first six years of the "Irish exile," between 1714 and 1720. Delany, who unlike these two authors had known Swift during the period in question, placed the writing "some years after" 1720.[3] No evidence to resolve these conflicting views came to light until 1935, when Professor Nichol Smith published the letters of Swift to Charles Ford, with some letters of Bolingbroke to Ford as an appendix. These shed a great deal of new light on the problem, although it is perhaps going too far to say, as Professor Quintana does, that they leave it no longer a matter of conjecture. As a preliminary to further investigation, the pertinent passages from all the correspondence of Swift and his friends are printed here in chronological order.

Swift (in Dublin) to Ford (in London), April 15, 1721.

> I am now writing a History of my Travells, which will be a large Volume, and gives Account of Countryes hitherto unknown; but they go on slowly for want of Health and Humor.[4]

Bolingbroke (in Nogent-sur-Seine) to Swift, January 1, 1722 [N.S.]

> I long to see your Travels; for, take it as you will, I do not retract what I said, and will undertake to find, in two pages of your *bagatelles*, more good sense, useful knowledge, and true religion, than you can show me in the works of nineteen in twenty of the profound divines and philosophers of the age.[5]

Esther Vanhomrigh (in Dublin) to Swift (in the country), June, 1722.

One day this week I was to visit a great lady that has been a-travelling for some time past, where I found a very great assembly of ladies and beaux, dressed as I suppose to a nicety. I hope you will pardon me now I tell you that I heartily wished you a spectator, for I very much question if in your life you ever saw the like scene, or one more extraordinary. The lady's behaviour was blended with so many different characters, I cannot possibly describe it without tiring your patience. But the audience seemed to be a creation of her own, they were so very obsequious. Their forms and gestures were very like those of baboons and monkeys; they all grinned and chattered at the same time, and that of things I did not understand. The rooms being hung with arras, in which were trees very well described, just as I was considering their beauty, and wishing myself in the country with ————, one of these animals snatched my fan, and was so pleased with me, that it seized me with such a panic that I apprehended nothing less than being carried up to the top of the house and served as a friend of yours was, but in this ———— one of their own species came in, upon which they all began to make their grimaces, which opportunity I took and made my escape.[6]

Swift (in Loughall) to Esther Vanhomrigh, July 13, 1722.

The use I have made of it [bad weather] was to read I know not how many diverting books of history and travels.[7]

Swift to Ford (in Dublin), July 22, 1722.

The bad Weather has made me read through abundance of Trash, and this hath made me almost forget how to hold a Pen, which I must therefore keep for Dublin, Winter and Sickness.[8]

Bolingbroke (in Paris) to Ford (in London), December 25, 1723: sent by mistake to Swift (in Dublin).

thanks be to Stella! I will neither pun nor quibble, but I am confident that we had lost the Dean if it had not been for her. if she had not fix'd his course, our poor friend would have wander'd from one ideal world to another, and have forgot even the Species he is of. he had been att this very instant perhaps freezing in Saturn, burning in Mercury, or stalking along with a load on his back, a bell under his chin, a plume on his head, and a fox tail att each ear, in that country which he discover'd not long ago, where Horses and mules are the reasonable Creatures, and men the Beasts of burden. But thanks to heaven & Stella, that danger is over. since he loves a woman he will not forget that he is a man.[9]

Swift (in Dublin) to Ford (in London), January 19, 1723-4.

Last Night I received the Pacquet franckt *Osborn*. I suppose it is L[d] Caemarthen. I was at a Loss about one of the Letters, at first, but after found it was to you, and that you are a Traytor into the Bargain: else how should he know any Thing of Stella or of Horses. Tis hard that Folks in France will not let us in Ireland be quiet. I would have him and you know that I hate Yahoos of both Sexes, and that Stella and Madame de Vilette are onely tolerable at best, for want of Houyhnhnms. . . . My greatest want here is of somebody qualifyed to censure and correct what I write, I know not above two or three whose Judgment I would value, and they are lazy, negligent, and without any Opinion of my Abilityes. I have left the Country of Horses, and am in the flying Island, where I shall not stay long, and my two last Journyes will soon be over; so that if you come here this Summer you will find me returnd.[10]

Swift to Ford, February 13, 1723-4.

The letter [from Bolingbroke] to you is separate, if it be to you as I suppose. He thanks you for the few Lines added by you to the Letter I sent him, raillyes me upon my Southern Journey, says, and swears it is no Pun, That Stella fixed my Course, talks of the Houyhnhnms as if he were acquainted with him [them], and in that shows you as a most finished Traitor, for which you make very indifferent Excuses.[11]

Swift to Ford, April 2, 1724.

I shall have finished my Travells very soon if I have Health, Leisure, and humor.[12]

Bolingbroke (in France) to Swift, September 12 [N.S.], 1724.

You desire me to return home, and you promise me in that case to come to London, loaden with your Travels.[13]

Bolingbroke (in London) to Swift, July 24, 1725.

This much I thought I might say about my private affairs to
an old friend, without diverting him too long from his labours
to promote the advantage of the Church and State of Ireland;
or, from his travels into those countries of giants and pigmies,
from whence he imports a cargo I value at a higher rate than
that of the richest galleon.[14]

Swift (at Quilca) to Ford, August 14, 1725.

I have finished my Travells, and I am now transcribing
them; they are admirable Things, and will wonderfully mend
the World.[15]

Swift to Ford, August 16, 1725.

I am amusing my self in the Quality of Bayliff to Sheridan,
among Bogs and Rocks, overseeing and ranting at Irish La-
borers, reading Books twice over for want of fresh ones, and
fairly correcting and transcribing my Travells, for the Publick.[16]

Swift to Thomas Sheridan (in Dublin), September 11, 1725.

Therefore sit down and be quiet, and mind your business as
you should do, and contract your friendships, and expect no
more from man than such an animal is capable of, and you
will every day find my description of Yahoos more resembling.[17]

Pope (in Twickenham) to Swift, September 14, 1725.

Your Travels I hear much of; my own, I promise you shall
never more be in a strange land, but a diligent, I hope useful
investigation of my own territories.[18]

Swift to Pope, September 29, 1725.

I have employed my time, besides ditching, in finishing, correcting, amending, and transcribing my Travels, in four parts
complete, newly augmented, and intended for the press, when
the world shall deserve them, or rather when a printer shall
be found brave enough to venture his ears. I like the scheme of
our meeting after distresses and dispersions; but the chief end
I propose to myself in all my labours is to vex the world rather
than divert it; and if I could compass that design, without
hurting my own person or fortune, I would be the most inde-
fatigable writer you have ever seen, without reading. I am

exceedingly pleased that you have done with translations. Lord Treasurer Oxford often lamented that a rascally world should lay you under a necessity of mis-employing your genius for so long a time. But since you will now be so much better employed, when you think of the world give it one lash the more at my request. I have ever hated all nations, professions, and communities, and all my love is toward individuals: for instance, I hate the tribe of lawyers, but I love Counsellor Such-a-one, and Judge Such-a-one: so with physicians—I will not speak of my own trade—soldiers, English, Scotch, French, and the rest. But principally I hate and detest that animal called man, although I heartily love John, Peter, Thomas, and so forth. This is the system upon which I have governed myself many years, but do not tell, and so I shall go on till I have done with them. I have got materials toward a treatise, proving the falsity of that definition *animal rationale,* and to show it would be only *rationis capax.* Upon this great foundation of misanthropy, though not in Timon's manner, the whole building of my Travels is erected; and I never will have peace of mind till all honest men are of my opinion. By consequence you are to embrace it immediately, and procure that all who deserve my esteem may do so too. The matter is so clear that it will admit of no dispute; nay, I will hold a hundred pounds that you and I agree in the point. . . .

Mr. Lewis sent me an account of Dr. Arbuthnot's illness, which is a very sensible affliction to me, who, by living so long out of the world, have lost that hardness of heart contracted by years and general conversation. I am daily losing friends, and neither seeking nor getting others. Oh! if the world had but a dozen Arbuthnots in it, I would burn my Travels.[19]

Arbuthnot (in London) to Swift, October 17, 1725.

As for your book, of which I have framed to myself such an idea, that I am persuaded there is no doing any good upon mankind without it, I will set the letters myself, rather than that it should not be published. But before you put the finishing hand to it, it is really necessary to be acquainted with some new improvements of mankind, that have appeared of late, and are daily appearing. Mankind has an inexhaustible source of invention in the way of folly and madness.[20]

Swift to Pope, November 26, 1725.

I tell you after all, that I do not hate mankind: it is *vous autres* who hate them, because you would have them reasonable animals, and are angry for being disappointed. I have always rejected that definition, and made another of my own. I am no more angry with [Walpole] than I was with the kite that last week flew away with one of my chickens; and yet I was pleased when one of my servants shot him two days after. This I say, because you are so hardy as to tell me of your intentions to write maxims in opposition to Rochefoucauld, who is my favourite, because I found my whole character in him. However I will read him again, because it is possible I may have since undergone some alterations.[21]

Bolingbroke to Swift, December 14, 1725.

Pope and you are very great wits, and I think very indifferent philosophers. If you despised the world as much as you pretend, and perhaps believe, you would not be so angry with it. The founder of your sect, that noble original whom you think it so great an honour to resemble, was a slave to the worst part of the world, to the Court; and all his big words were the language of a slighted lover, who desired nothing so much as a reconciliation, and feared nothing so much as a rupture. I believe the world has used me as scurvily as most people, and yet I could never find in my heart to be thoroughly angry with the simple, false, capricious thing. I should blush alike to be discovered fond of the world, or piqued at it. Your definition of *animal capax rationis*, instead of the common one *animal rationale*, will not bear examination: define but reason, and you will see why your distinction is no better than that of the pontiff Cotta, between *mala ratio* and *bona ratio*.[22]

The first of these passages from the correspondence effectually disposes of the contention that *Gulliver's Travels* had been completed by 1720. Yet it has not entirely destroyed the belief that parts of the book were composed as early as 1714. The currently accepted theory, subscribed to by so many Swiftians that it may be called the orthodox theory, runs somewhat as follows. Swift began parts of the book in 1714 as contributions to the works of Martinus Scriblerus. What now constitutes the first, second, and sixth chapters of the

Voyage to Lilliput was originally intended as a rather light-hearted parody of travel literature. Another unfinished composition, a burlesque of experimental science, eventually became the fifth and sixth chapters of the Voyage to Laputa. The incorporation of these passages into Gulliver produced an inconsistency of tone and purpose in the first and third voyages, as contrasted with the homogeneity of the voyages to Brobdingnag and to the land of the Houyhnhnms.[23]

The proponents of this theory rely principally upon a passage in Spence's anecdotes. "It was from a part of these memoirs [of Scriblerus] that Dr. Swift took his first hints for *Gulliver*," Pope told Spence about 1730. "There were pigmies in Schreibler's *Travels*, and the projects of Laputa."[24] The phraseology of this statement is interesting. Not only does Pope *not* say that Swift wrote these portions of the *Memoirs*, but he asserts that Swift took hints from them. It is unusual to speak of a man taking hints from himself. Moreover, the Club seems to have recognized that Arbuthnot was the appropriate satirist where ridicule of false scientific learning was concerned. Swift himself took this position in a letter sent to Arbuthnot on July 3, 1714, a month after Swift had begun the dispersal of the Club by withdrawing from London to Letcombe. In response to an admonition by the doctor to "remember Martin" in his retirement, Swift replied:

> To talk of Martin in any hands but yours, is a folly. You every day give better hints than all of us together could do in a twelvemonth; and to say the truth, Pope who first thought of the hint has no genius at all to it, in my mind. Gay is too young; Parnell has some ideas of it, but is idle; I could put together, and lard, and strike out well enough, but all that relates to the sciences must be from you.[25]

A year later, apparently in reply to a suggestion by Pope, he wrote the latter, ". . . truly I must be a little easy in my mind before I can think of Scriblerus."[26] And finally, after the publication of the *Travels*, Gay and Pope, in a joint letter dated November 17, 1726, reported Arbuthnot as saying it was "ten thousand pities he had not known it [*Gulliver*], he could have added such abundance of things upon every subject."[27]

This 'statement, of course, cannot be taken literally, but in conjunction with Arbuthnot's own remark in his letter to Swift nine days earlier, that "the part of the projectors is the least brilliant," it would seem to indicate that the doctor did not recognize any old Scriblerian material in Gulliver, and possibly that he had not had an opportunity to examine the manuscript.

Another important fact to be considered is the existence of passages in the *Memoirs of Scriblerus*, as they were published in 1741, which accord perfectly with Pope's remark to Spence. *An Essay of the Learned Martinus Scriblerus, Concerning the Origine of Sciences* contains the following paragraph:

> Nor Troy nor Thebes were the first of Empires; we have mention, tho' not histories, of an earlier warlike people call'd the Pygmæans. I cannot but persuade my self, from those Accounts of Homer, Aristotle and others, of their history, wars, and revolutions, and from the very Air in which those authors speak of them as of things known, that they were then a part of the study of the Learned. And tho' all we directly hear is of their Military atchievments in the brave defence of their country from the annual invasions of a powerful enemy yet I cannot doubt but that they excell'd as much in the arts of peaceful government, tho' there remain no traces of their civil institutions. . . . Nothing is more natural to imagine, than that the few survivors of that empire retired into the depths of their Deserts, where they lived undisturb'd, 'till they were found out by Osyris, in his travels to instruct mankind.[28]

The authors of the *Essay Concerning the Origine of Sciences*, as Pope informed Spence,[29] were Arbuthnot, Pope, and Parnell, and as Parnell died in 1718, we seem to have here a part of the early work of the Club. Pope, when he edited the uncompleted works of Scriblerus for publication, inserted a chapter in order to claim *Gulliver's Travels* as a part of the grand design. "Thou shalt know then, that in his first Voyage he [Martinus] was carry'd by a prosperous Storm, to a Discovery of the Remains of the ancient *Pygmæan* Empire."[30] The verbal echo of the paragraph quoted from the *Essay* is striking evidence to identify it as the source from which

Pope believed Swift took his hint for the voyage to Lilliput.

It is even easier to find in the *Memoirs* of Scriblerus passages which might have supplied Swift with "hints" for the projects of Laputa. The eighth, tenth, eleventh, and twelfth chapters abound with hare-brained schemes and experiments. It is generally agreed that these are the work of Arbuthnot. The external evidence, therefore, is against, rather than for, the orthodox theory that part of *Gulliver's Travels* consists of recast material originally written for the Scriblerus Club.

The internal evidence for the theory is the alleged inconsistency in tone of the first voyage and the incoherence of the third. The latter question can be taken up most profitably along with the discussion of the general structure of the *Travels*. The former argument depends on a presumption based on insufficient external evidence. For, examined without prejudice, the first two chapters of Gulliver appear to be a perfectly natural introduction to the story under cover of which Swift intends to shoot his wit: moreover, they contain events which are a necessary part of the political allegory. These introductory chapters are neither more or less imaginative, or more or less closely linked with the main purpose of the book, than are the corresponding chapters of the second voyage, which, if they show a slight deepening in tone, do so in accord with Swift's intention to deepen the character of his principal figure as an integral part of his main design.

What, then, is the main design of *Gulliver's Travels*? It is customary to call the book a satire: it would be more accurate and more illuminating to call it a politico-sociological treatise much of which is couched in the medium of satire. Only secondarily and accidentally is it a book of travels. It belongs with the *Utopia*, the *New Atlantis*, *Candide*, and *Erewhon*: it succeeds in combining the depth of the two earlier tales with the narrative skill and human appeal of the two later. And it is perhaps not surprising that many people in Swift's age, unaccustomed to so much brilliant embroidering of a serious philosophic theme, as well as unwilling to face the underlying indictment of European civilization, should have defended themselves, half unconsciously, by construing Gulliver as an amusing, imaginative romance marred by some regrettable misanthropic passages.

If the theory of a patchwork *Gulliver*, springing from Scriblerus, is abandoned, it becomes necessary to inquire anew what put the idea of the *Travels* into Swift's mind, and precisely when he began to plan them and to begin the actual writing. These are problems yet unsolved and probably insoluble, although it is possible to hazard a few conjectures. For nearly six years after his departure from England in 1714 Swift spent almost all of his energies in the reformation of the affairs of St. Patrick's Cathedral: he wrote nothing, or next to nothing, for publication. In May, 1720, however, there appeared in Dublin a pamphlet entitled *A Proposal for the Universal Use of Irish Manufacture*, attacking English laws which restricted Irish trade. It was the first of the great series of Swift's patriotic writings of which the most famous and most powerful were to be the *Drapier's Letters* four years later. The series is, however, by no means regular. For over a year Swift seems to have concentrated upon this new activity and the controversies which it aroused—controversies which included the prosecution by the government of the printer of the first pamphlet, with obvious threatening implications toward the author, whose identity was an open secret. It seems hardly likely that this affair could have left very much opportunity for Swift to devise and begin to execute an important literary project. But in 1721 the litigation over the *Proposal* languished and the pamphlets became less frequent. It is natural to infer not only that the writing of the patriotic pamphlets had destroyed Swift's literary inertia, but that they may have had even more to do with inspiring Gulliver, though not as a part of the Irish series. The events which underlay the increased oppression of Ireland by England were of at least equal importance for England, and Swift had by no means lost his interest in English politics or his hope for the restoration to power of what was, to him, the "right" party. Six years of Whig administration had now culminated in the bursting of the South Sea Bubble—a scandal great enough to satisfy the expectations of the most ardent Tory. Swift must

have seen in this catastrophe the justification of his own
political theories and the opportunity for his reentry into the
larger world of European affairs. He begins to show renewed
interest in his English public in the fall of 1720:[31] quite possibly we may date the conception of Gulliver early in that fall,
when the significance of the South Sea debacle was becoming
evident. And since Swift writes to Ford on April 15, 1721,[32]
that he is actually engaged upon the *Travels*, we can hardly be
far wrong if we assume that he commenced them about the
beginning of that year.

It is not difficult to see why Swift, having determined to
write his politico-sociological treatise, should have chosen to
cast it in the form of a travel book. In a sense its two most
famous predecessors, the *Utopia* and the *New Atlantis*, were
also travel books. The greater emphasis by Swift on the
element of travel description may easily be accounted for by
his long-standing interest in this sort of literature, and by his
desire to burlesque certain features of it. It is a temptation to
suggest that one specific travel book had something to do
with Swift's decision. In the fall of 1720 *Robinson Crusoe*
had been published just a year: so widely read a tale can
hardly have escaped Swift's notice. But Swift seems to have
paid little attention to Defoe, and superficial parallels between
Crusoe and the *Travels* (such, for example, as occur in the
opening paragraphs of the two books) are not close enough
or distinctive enough to warrant anything more than a pious
hope that there may have been some slight connection between
the two most famous stories of their day.

The theories of politics and society which prompted Swift
to write *Gulliver's Travels* were those which, with very minor
changes, he held all his life, so far as we have any record.
They are expressed in his first political pamphlet, *A Discourse
of the Contests and Dissensions Between the Nobles and the
Commons in Athens and Rome*, published in 1701. They are
reaffirmed in a letter directed by Swift to Pope, dated January 10 (probably 1721-2),[33] and obviously intended as a formal *apologia* for his public career. The letter is too long for

reproduction here, but it should be read by every student of Swift and his works.

The basis of Swift's political theory was contained in the principles of the old Whigs, of whom Sir William Temple was an eminent spokesman. Authority was held to reside in the whole of the body politic, though the administrative power, for practical reasons, had to be delegated to a small number of persons; perhaps, under certain circumstances, to one. The three estates of the realm—king, nobles, and commons—were of equal importance to the state, the king being charged with keeping the balance between the others. This form of government was frequently called the "gothic": it was assumed to be the natural, primitive government of the old English, and deviations from it were held to be corruptions. These deviations were always the result of an attempt by one of the estates to seize more than its share of the power for selfish reasons: if this attempt was successful it was inevitable that disturbances would result which would ultimately culminate in tyranny by one of the estates. This in turn would be done away with, after much suffering, and the old balance would be reestablished. It was the duty of intelligent men to preserve the balance as long as possible, and to restore it whenever it was destroyed.

The position of the church in such a state was, naturally, of great importance to Swift. He believed firmly in both the truth of the religion of which he was a priest and the propriety of its establishment as the state religion of England and Ireland. But he did not believe either that dissenters from the state church should be prevented from worshiping in accordance with their consciences, or that the church or its members should rebel against the constituted authority of the temporal government within the scope of its operations. His position was that of a moderate, reasonable Englishman who never found himself far out of agreement with the less extreme members of either party.

If the sincerity and depth of Swift's belief in these principles is once understood it is not difficult to explain what has sometimes been regarded as a turning of his political coat in or about the year 1710. Swift always insisted that he remained steadfast in his beliefs and that it was the parties that altered their creeds: history supports him in this. During his youth in Ireland the Tory party was associated with the theory of the divine right of the king over both church and state, and with the consequent threat of the reestablishment of Roman Catholicism. This seemed to Swift an instance of that tyranny which it was right for honest and intelligent men to destroy in order to restore the power to the whole rather than to a part of the state. Accordingly he subscribed to "revolution principles" (which, incidentally, he maintained even after his secession to the Tories, though many of his new associates publicly or privately repudiated them). But when the more radical Whigs began to urge the repeal of the sacramental test, in order that dissenters might hold places in the government, he became estranged from the party. Eventually he was convinced that the Tories, who upheld the test and resisted the tendency of the Whigs to weaken the power of the sovereign and place all authority in Parliament, were now the champions of sound governmental practice. This feeling accounts for the energy with which he attacked Steele for his unlucky statement that the country "expected" Queen Anne to do something about Dunkirk. With the death of Anne and the accession of the House of Hanover the Whigs' desire to circumscribe the power of the crown became still more marked, and the Bangorian controversy brought to a head a similar Whig policy with regard to the power of the state church.

At first sight it may seem odd that Swift, if he wrote *Gulliver's Travels* as a treatise on political theory, should have paid so little attention to ecclesiastical affairs. There are several possible explanations for his course. In the first place, both for his own sake and that of the church, the welfare of which was now one of his chief concerns, Swift probably had no intention of including in his satire anything which would give his enemies renewed grounds for accusing him of blasphemy, as they had done ever since the publication of *A Tale of a Tub*. Secondly, the introduction of religion into the *Travels* would have complicated an already complex design, and perhaps have focused more attention upon specific local questions than Swift would have wished in a book which he meant to apply to the world at large.

When the politico-sociological nature of the *Travels* is once clearly understood, the structure of the book, though complex, is easier to analyze. Each of the four voyages approaches the main problem in a different way. For the sake of variety there is an alternation between the negative and the positive statement of principles. The first and third voyages are chiefly attacks upon the evils of bad government, the second and fourth are expositions of good government. This accounts for both the dominant satiric tone of the voyages to Lilliput and Laputa, and the frequency in them of topical allusions. Over this fundamental design is superimposed another. The first two voyages are carefully contrasted: the first, or negative one depicts a typical European government which has become more corrupt than the average, while the second, or positive one portrays a government better than the average. In neither case does Swift proceed to extremes: he seems to be trying to show the range within which, humanity being what it is, actual governments may be expected to move. Lilliput has some good features, Brobdingnag some bad. The reader gets the impression that while Swift the idealist would not be contented with Brobdingnag, Swift the realist would grudgingly accept it. It represents, perhaps, England as it could be made within his own lifetime if by some happy turn of the wheel the country might be put into the hands of himself and his friends. To reinforce this relationship between the voyages Swift not only employed the contrasting devices of pigmies and giants, but even constructed the two voyages, roughly, on the same pattern. In each case Gulliver gives the name of the ship in which he embarks, the name of the master, and circumstantial details of the voyage and of the manner in which he arrives, companionless, in an unknown land. In each case he falls first into the hands of common inhabitants of the country, who turn him over to persons of higher position. Then follow details of his temporary discomforts in the hands of these people, including scatological incidents apparently motivated in part by a desire to burlesque the habits of travel writers who assume that the most trivial occurrences in which they have been involved must be of interest to their readers. Next comes the manner of Gulliver's introduction to the Court, with descriptions of the ruler, his wife, the capital city of the kingdom, and one or more of the most striking buildings. About three-quarters of the way through each voyage comes a chapter largely devoted to discussing distinctive and unusual customs of the country. Near the end of the voyage Gulliver leaves the capital and, as a result, manages in the last chapter to escape and to be picked up by a vessel which carries him back to England. Each voyage concludes with Gulliver's reunion with his family.

If the design of the *Travels* were absolutely symmetrical, one might expect to find a connection between the last two voyages corresponding to that between the first two. This, however, is not the case. Having shown bad and good government as they actually exist, or might exist, Swift wished also to show ideally good government as he conceived it. Instead of presenting a contrasting ideally bad state in a separate voyage, he preferred to combine the two extremes in a single climactic book. This course not only made the contrast between the two ideals more vivid, but also made it possible for Swift's ideally good Houyhnhnms to understand the nature of evil, which would otherwise have been beyond their comprehension. The third voyage was therefore devoted to a second description of bad government *in esse*. It was not, however, an extension or repetition of the first voyage, but a complement to it. All of his life Swift blamed the misfortunes of mankind upon two causes, vice and folly, both of which were contrary to right reason, and either of which could destroy a state. In the first voyage he had emphasized the former cause: in the third voyage he concentrated upon the latter.

It is important to keep in mind the main purpose of this third voyage, which has universally been judged to be the least successful of the four, largely for lack of unity. It is impossible not to agree with the general verdict, but it is easy to overstate the degree of disorganization. Superficially the voyage seems to be divided into four sections, recounting the adventures in Laputa, in Balnibarbi, in Glubbdubdrib, and in Luggnagg. The first two sections are regarded as attacks upon science, the third as a criticism of history, and the fourth as a personal expression of Swift's fear of old age. In point of fact, the attacks upon science and history are subsidiary to a single main purpose—an attack upon folly in government, which, in Swift's view, was identical with theoretical innovation, as opposed to the following of old and tried methods, modified only by the adoption of such variations as have been proved successful in practice in other countries. Swift apparently felt that the Whigs had transferred to the scientists much of the encouragement which earlier administrations had given to men of letters, and he regarded this tendency as symptomatic of the inclination of the Whigs toward chimerical experimentation in all fields.

The attack on the "pure" sciences of mathematics, astronomy, and music was probably associated most closely with the inner court circle in Laputa because Swift felt that it was the practitioners of these arts who had the ear of George I. Handel was enjoying royal patronage, Flamsteed and Halley had been given numerous grants, including Flamsteed House in Greenwich (the beginning of the Royal Observatory), and Isaac Newton had not only been knighted, but had been called in as an expert to support the Whig administration's contention that Wood's halfpence were not debased coins. This, naturally, enraged Swift: it is quite possibly at the root of his observation about the fondness of mathematicians for meddling in politics:

> But, what I chiefly admired, and thought altogether unaccountable, was the strong Disposition I observed in them towards News and Politicks, perpetually enquiring into Publick Affairs, giving their Judgments in matters of State; and passionately disputing every Inch of a Party Opinion. I have indeed observed the same Disposition among most of the Mathematicians I have known in *Europe*, although I could never discover the least Analogy between the two Sciences; unless those People suppose, that because the smallest Circle

hath as many Degrees as the largest, therefore the Regulation and Management of the World require no more Abilities than the handling and turning of a Globe. But, I rather take this Quality to spring from a very common Infirmity of Human Nature, inclining us to be more curious and conceited in Matters where we have least Concern, and for which we are least adapted either by Study or Nature. (3.2.12.)

The activities of the "projectors" or inventors in the field of applied science are satirized in the description of the activities of Balnibarbi. The picture of agricultural conditions in the subject island, culminating in Munodi's story of the old and the new mills, is, as has already been pointed out, an allegorical criticism of the new Whig economic and financial policies. In the Grand Academy of Lagado it is not only in the school of political projectors that Swift has statecraft in his mind: even in the fifth chapter the experiments, on analysis, will be found to constitute absurd attempts, fostered by the government, to alter the normal mode of life within the country. Often the ultimate purposes of these experiments are quite practical, but the methods by which the purposes are to be achieved are too roundabout, too expensive, and utterly unlikely to bring about the end in view.

In contrast with all this are the examples of good government in accordance with the tried, sound principles of ancient models, as described by the ghosts of Glubbdubdrib. The exemplar of "gothic" government in classical times is the Roman republic at its best. The great heroes are the two Brutuses and the younger Cato, and the Roman senate is described as "an Assembly of Heroes and Demy-Gods." Julius Caesar and the succeeding emperors are treated as tyrants, under whose rule corruption and luxury brought about the decay of all virtues. More than once modern European governments are likened to those of imperial Rome: the disappearance of "*Roman* Virtue" is lamented, and the British Parliament, under a thin disguise, is described as "a Knot of Pick-pockets, High-waymen and Bullies." (3.7.8.)

The account of the struldbruggs near the end of the third voyage is the episode which, more than any other in the

Travels, seems to be dissociated from the main scheme of the book. It is often spoken of as a purely personal expression by Swift of his fear of senility. That this personal feeling intensified the author's emotions as he wrote the passage no one can doubt: nevertheless the incident is logically related to the purpose of the voyage. It will be remembered that Gulliver interrupts the Luggnaggian's first description of the struldbruggs with a rhapsody in which he allows his mind to speculate on the happiness which must be the lot of these immortal creatures and the benefits which their ever-increasing experience and wisdom must confer upon the rest of mankind. The reaction of the gentlemen of Luggnagg with whom Gulliver is talking is significant.

> When I had ended, and the Sum of my Discourse had been interpreted as before, to the rest of the Company, there was a good deal of Talk among them in the Language of the Country, not without some Laughter at my Expence. At last the same Gentleman who had been my Interpreter said, he was desired by the rest to set me right in a few Mistakes, which I had fallen into through the common Imbecillity of human Nature, and upon that allowance was less answerable for them. (3.10.11.)

The whole chapter is one more rebuke to human folly which, giving itself over to wishful thinking, conjures up imaginary and impossible ways of dealing with the ills of society, instead of recognizing the nature of mankind as it is and approaching human problems from a practical point of view.

Swift's decision to cast his treatise in the form of a narrative necessitated the creation of a protagonist. Gulliver is all too often identified with Swift himself. No single misinterpretation of Swift's intentions has done more to obscure the real purpose of *Gulliver's Travels*. Gulliver is not only a character distinct from his creator—he is not identifiable with any of the actual contemporaries whose vicissitudes sometimes, especially in the first voyage, serve as a basis for his adventures. His birth, training, and early activities are carefully calculated to make him the perfect observer of and commentator upon the civilizations with which he comes in contact. By birth he is the average middle-class Englishman, with an inclination toward the sea, and with a special aptitude for languages which is to stand him in good stead. His education is more rounded than that of most men of his day: upon a base of traditional classical training as prescribed in the universities is superimposed the scientific training of the physician. A naturally studious habit leads him to supplement this training with much reading: adventurousness, curiosity, a faculty for observation and analysis of human nature and customs, and, most important, a high regard for truth, complete the mental and moral equipment of the perfect travel author.

But the Gulliver thus created is not a static character. When, at the age of about thirty-eight, he sets out on the voyage which is to bring him the first of his great adventures, he is temperamentally the typical English traveler of modern fiction, with an amused and superior toleration for the customs of foreign countries, tempered occasionally with a half-surprised admission that something might be said in favor of a few of these odd ways. Gulliver's experiences in Lilliput make no perceptible impression on his chauvinism, or on his love of his native country. His encounter with the ship which carries him back to England occasions an unusually fervent expression of this patriotism.

> It is not easy to express the Joy I was in upon the unexpected hope of once more seeing my beloved Country, and the dear Pledges I left in it. The ship slackned her Sails, and I came up with her between five and six in the Evening, *September* 26; but my Heart leapt within me to see her *English* Colours. (1.8.9.)

The voyage to Brobdingnag brings about the first alteration in Gulliver's general complacency over European civilization. In the third chapter he is made to feel uneasy by the amused contempt of the King and the courtiers for his country and countrymen as he describes them. But it is in the famous sixth chapter that we find Gulliver really on the defensive for the first time. The grand climax of this chapter is, of course, the judgment of the King in response to Gulliver's long and careful account of Europe and its inhabitants.

My little friend *Grildrig*; you have made a most admirable Panegyrick upon your Country. You have clearly proved that Ignorance, Idleness and Vice are the proper Ingredients for qualifying a Legislator. That Laws are best explained, interpreted, and applied by those whose Interest and Abilities lye in perverting, confounding, and eluding them. I observe among you some Lines of an Institution, which in its Original might have been tolerable, but these half erased, and the rest wholly blurred and blotted by Corruptions. It doth not appear from all you have said, how any one Virtue is required towards the Procurement of any one Station among you, much less that Men are ennobled on Account of their Virtue, that Priests are advanced for their Piety or Learning, Soldiers for their Conduct or Valour, Judges for their Integrity, Senators for the Love of their Country, or Counsellors for their Wisdom. As for yourself (continued the King) who have spent the greatest part of your Life in travelling, I am well disposed to hope you may hitherto have escaped many Vices of your Country. But, by what I have gathered from your own Relation, and the Answers I have with much Pains wringed and extorted from you, I cannot but conclude the Bulk of your Natives, to be the most pernicious Race of little odious Vermin that Nature ever suffered to crawl upon the Surface of the Earth. (2.6.18.)

Even more revealing of the change in Gulliver's character, and of his dawning consciousness that Europe may not, after all, be quite the picture of perfection he has always assumed it to be, is his statement at the beginning of the chapter which follows.

Nothing but an extreme Love of Truth could have hindred me from concealing this part of my Story. It was in vain to discover my Resentments, which were always turned into Ridicule; And I was forced to rest with Patience while my noble and most beloved Country was so injuriously treated. I am heartily sorry as any of my Readers can possibly be, that such an Occasion was given: but this Prince happened to be so curious and inquisitive upon every Particular, that it could not consist either with Gratitude or good Manners to refuse giving him what Satisfaction I was able. Yet thus much I may be allowed to say in my own Vindication, that I artfully eluded many of his Questions, and gave to every Point a more favourable turn by many Degrees than the strictness of Truth would allow. For, I have always born that laudable Partiality to my own Country, which *Dionysius Halicarnassensis* with so much Justice recommends to an Historian. I would hide the Frailties and Deformities of my Political Mother, and place her Virtues and Beauties in the most advantageous Light. This was my sincere Endeavour in those many Discourses I had with that mighty Monarch, although it unfortunately failed of Success. (2.7.1.)

It is not surprising that while Gulliver is anxious to escape from Brobdingnag, where he suffers daily indignities, he exhibits only a modified rapture upon his return to England.

In the third voyage Gulliver's emotions may be described as at a dead center. He appears to be cured of any extravagant admiration of European society : he has now become the detached and half-cynical commentator on human life from without. In this voyage alone he is an observer and not an actor. This is entirely appropriate to the development of his character, although it weakens the interest of the narrative and is, in fact, one of the most important reasons for the relative ineffectiveness of the voyage. Gulliver is coolly ironic in comparing Europe with Laputa, sometimes to the advantage of one, sometimes to that of the other, but in neither case with any show of partisanship. His comments upon his return to his country are the briefest and least emotional of the *Travels*. The opening paragraph of the last book speaks of his remaining at home "in a very happy condition" about four months, but this statement is for the purpose of providing a contrast with Gulliver's change of heart during the final voyage—a change of heart more significant and more carefully depicted than any that has gone before.

The changing attitude of Gulliver toward the yahoos and the Houyhnhnms is of the first importance in determining the significance of those two species and, in consequence, of the whole voyage—indeed, of the entire *Travels*. At the opening of the voyage Gulliver is a representative European, somewhat better, perhaps, than most of his class, but by no means a paragon, and certainly a man who has adjusted himself to a consciousness of the ordinary and even the extraordinary vices and follies of humanity. In this state he does not recognize that the yahoos have any likeness to man: they are, to him, "ugly Monsters," to be described as a traveler would describe any curious and loathesome beast he encountered in the course of his adventures. It is not until the Houyhnhnms place him beside a yahoo for purposes of comparison that he sees any resemblance between himself and these "abominable Animals," and then he emphasizes those physical aspects which the yahoos have in common with "savage Nations." At the same time he stresses the difference between the behavior of Europeans and that of yahoos, which is apparently something more repulsive than he has encountered in the whole breadth of his travels. For a considerable time he protests against being identified with the yahoos, and even begs his master not to apply the word "yahoo" to him. During the first three chapters he avoids speaking of Europeans as yahoos, calling them "others of my own Kind," "Creatures like myself," or "our Countrymen." Acknowledging the physical resemblance between human beings and yahoos, he protests that he cannot account for the "degenerate and brutal nature" of the latter. Gradually, in the course of the conversations with his master which occupy the fourth, fifth, sixth, and seventh chapters, Gulliver falls into the habit of referring to Europeans as yahoos, partly for convenience and partly because, as the perfection of the Houyhnhnms is borne in upon him and contrasted with the actions and thoughts of his countrymen, he becomes aware, little by little, of the discrepancy between ideal and actual man. This new consciousness is intensified by his contemplation of the Houyhnhnms and their institutions, as they are described in the eighth and ninth chapters. The ultimate state of mind produced in Gulliver by this gradual process of education through contact with a superior race is expressly stated in the tenth chapter.

At first, indeed, I did not feel that natural Awe which the *Yahoos* and all other Animals bear towards them; but it grew upon me by Degrees, much sooner than I imagined, and was mingled with a respectful Love and Gratitude, that they would

condescend to distinguish me from the rest of my Species.
(4.10.3.)

The attitude of the Houyhnhnms toward Gulliver is of
particular interest. From the first they distinguish him from
the yahoos of the island—partly, it is true, because of his
clothes, but also because of his behavior. The master Houyhnhnm at once admits Gulliver to the house, a privilege which he
would not have accorded an ordinary yahoo, and is astonished
at the "Teachableness, Civility and Cleanliness" of this
prodigy. All the Houyhnhnms who meet Gulliver are similarly impressed. The master describes him to the quadrennial
assembly as a "wonderful *Yahoo*" with all the qualities of that
animal, "only a little more civilized by some Tincture of Reason, which however was in a degree as far inferior to the
Houyhnhnm Race as the *Yahoos* of their Country were to
[Gulliver]." This placing of Gulliver midway between the
Houyhnhnms and the yahoos, by a creature possessing absolute accuracy of judgment, is extremely significant. In the end
the master dismisses Gulliver with regret and shows no disinclination to his society. In other words, a somewhat-above-
average Englishman was not altogether unacceptable company for a perfect being.

The natural result of Gulliver's experiences among the
Houyhnhnms, and of his mental development, is to be found
in the last two chapters of the *Travels* and in the *Letter to
Sympson*. The expressions about humanity which are found
here are not those of Gulliver in his normal state of mind.
Swift is employing a device which he has used once before, at
the conclusion of the second voyage, when his hero returned
from the earlier and less nearly perfect Utopia of Brobdingnag. Evidently Swift was fascinated by the idea of the difficulty of readjusting oneself to ordinary existence after a
prolonged exposure to extraordinary conditions. In the second voyage the extraordinary conditions have to do with
physical dimensions: and Swift, delighting in the play of his
imagination, spends nearly half of the last chapter in describing Gulliver's inability to accustom himself to the size of the

captain and crew of the ship which rescues him, and his odd behavior on his arrival in England.

> As I was on the Road, observing the Littleness of the Houses, the Trees, the Cattle and the People, I began to think my self in *Lilliput*. I was afraid of trampling on every Traveller I met, and often called aloud to have them stand out of the way, so that I had like to have gotten one or two broken Heads for my Impertinence.
>
> When I came to my own House, for which I was forced to enquire, one of the Servants opening the Door, I bent down to go in (like a Goose under a Gate) for fear of striking my Head. My Wife ran out to embrace me, but I stooped lower than her Knees, thinking she could otherwise never be able to reach my Mouth. My Daughter kneeled to ask me Blessing, but I could not see her till she arose, having been so long used to stand with my Head and Eyes erect to above sixty Foot; and then I went to take her up with one Hand, by the Waste. I looked down upon the Servants and one or two Friends who were in the House, as if they had been Pigmies, and I a Giant. I told my Wife she had been too thrifty, for I found she had starved herself and her Daughter to nothing. In short, I behaved my self so unaccountably, that they were all of the Captain's Opinion when he first saw me, and concluded I had lost my Wits. This I mention as an Instance of the great Power of Habit and Prejudice. (2.8.15-16.)

In the same way, but dealing with a far more significant matter—readjustment to mental and spiritual, rather than physical conditions—Swift shows us at the end of the fourth voyage his conception of the effects which would be produced in the mind of an intelligent man who spent a long period in the company of creatures who were perfect in every way. Such a man, Swift believed, would tend to exaggerate his own imperfections and those of the race to which he belonged, and would, in the end, find living with his former associates intolerable. Anything less than perfection would be abhorrent: degrees of imperfection would be imperceptible and irrelevant. The opinions concerning mankind which Gulliver gives vent to are his own, not those of his creator. To emphasize this, Swift provides Gulliver with an unusual rescuer from his last adventure—Captain Pedro de Mendez. The majority of the seamen in the *Travels* are a good sort, but Mendez is a paragon. His generosity, his acute perception of the state of Gulliver's mind, his unfailing kindliness in the face of repeated rebuffs, mark him as the finest of all the European characters in the book. Yet Gulliver, controlled by the exalted conception of virtue he has acquired from living with Houyhnhnms, and by his now fixed belief in the utter worthlessness of all yahoos, with whom he has come to group the human race, is unable to perceive even the most extraordinary goodness when it manifests itself in one of the hated species. The effects of this mental alteration are, of course, more lasting than those which resulted from the journey to Brobdingnag, but they are not permanent: after five years Gulliver is able in retrospect to appreciate the virtues of Mendez (4.11.14), and he gradually becomes more accustomed to his family (4.12.12). The *Letter to Sympson* is a flare-up of the old idealism: it is also Swift's attempt to do the almost impossible—to write a second climax to his book more powerful than the first.

Parallel with the deepening of Gulliver's character run other literary devices which reinforce it. The most interesting of these has to do with the events leading up to his various adventures. In the first case he suffers shipwreck, caused by sheer mischance, or at the most mischance combined with natural human carelessness. On his arrival in Brobdingnag he is deserted by his terrified comrades under circumstances which make their cowardice understandable and perhaps excusable. At the beginning of the third voyage he experiences violence and cruelty from pirates. Finally he is marooned on Houyhnhnmland by the treachery of his own men. So effective a progression can hardly have been the result of accident.

There is plenty of other evidence of the careful planning and equally careful revision of the book before publication. Swift's first reference to the *Travels* in his letters to Ford[34] indicates that the large design was already clear in his mind in April, 1721. Apparently he devoted from fourteen to seventeen months to the draft of the first two voyages,[35] and a year and a half to the fourth[36] (the latter period, near its end, being disturbed by the culmination of the affair of Vanessa). It is interesting to find that he composed the third voyage last, evidently feeling that the main theme was chiefly developed in the others: yet as he embarked upon the third voyage he wrote to Ford in words which show that he had previously conveyed to his friend the plan he intended to follow.[37] The writing of the third voyage (interrupted by the *Drapier's Letters*) took another year and a half,[38] and finally he required more than half a year to correct, augment, and transcribe the whole of the *Travels*.[39] This hardly agrees with the theory that the four voyages show a lack of unified planning, and that their tone and subject matter indicate that they were the product of events which occurred while Swift was writing and of the moods which these events created in the author's mind. Indeed, it is strange that anyone familiar with Swift's political pamphlets of the last four years of Anne's reign, with their masterly adjustment of tone to the audience and to the end desired, should suppose that in his greatest work, over the composition and revision of which he spent far more time and pains than over any other of his books, he should have been the slave of passing moods.

Above all it is necessary to insist upon the fact that Swift never allowed specific incidents to interfere with his general purpose, though like most good authors he was quick to seize upon them when he could turn them to account. Dante, when he wished to rebuke the vices of his day, often inveighed against them in the persons of unimportant contemporaries. Swift, attacking the ignorance and ingratitude displayed by the public in its treatment of its leaders, drew upon the careers of two of his friends who were of unquestionable importance and who, he felt sincerely, had suffered from these vices of the populace. But Swift was more skillful than Dante at least in this: his readers might apprehend the full meaning of his sermon without bothering their heads about Oxford or Bolingbroke. The parable of the rebellion of Lindalino could carry its message, and can still carry it, to those who care nothing for eighteenth-century Dublin and Wood's brass money. Swift's use of this latter incident in *Gulliver's Travels* is the best example of his subordination of personal and local interests to his greater design. Had he been governed by an egotistic desire to exalt his own importance, what an opportunity this story afforded him! Had he been the Irishman prosecuting a war against England, how much he might have made of a sectional quarrel! But he was here concerned with the larger issue of tyranny over the whole British nation by a despotic king and his court. If there is an "Irish period" in Swift's writings it does not show itself in *Gulliver's Travels*, either here or in his picture of the yahoos, whom some would have to be "the old savage Irish." These miserable, mistreated people could, indeed, have furnished Swift with material for his physical description of the subhuman creatures so deeply detested by the Houyhnhnms, but so could the poorer classes in England, where crime, poverty, dirt, drunkenness and disease had not yet been done away with, as Hogarth's drawings testify. Swift, in his greatest work, had set up a larger canvas: his *atelier* was Ireland, his model England, his portrait that of western civilization. Of his purpose we have his own testimony both before and after the publication of Gulliver. Writing to Ford in 1725 he said his *Travels* were admirable things and would wonderfully mend the world. In the summer of 1727 the Abbé des Fontaines, who had translated the *Travels* into French, wrote to Swift apologizing for the omission of some passages not suitable for France. Swift replied,

> If the volumes of Gulliver were designed only for the British Isles, that traveler ought to pass for a very contemptible writer. The same vices and the same follies reign everywhere; at least in the civilized countries of Europe: and the author who writes only for one city, one province, one kingdom, or even one age, does not deserve to be read, let alone translated.[40]

The two passages just quoted emphasize a fact too often ignored by readers of *Gulliver's Travels*—that Swift conceived himself as a positive moral and social reformer. From his earliest to his latest writings there is plentiful evidence of his conviction that he knew not only what was wrong with the world, but also the means by which the world could be brought nearer to perfection. Living as he did in an age which was habituated to a belief that the world tended to decline, whether from the Golden Age of classical mythology or from the Garden of Eden of Hebrew legend, it is not surprising that he proposed reforms which often (though by no means always) called for a return to a real or an imagined earlier practice that was nearer to perfection. The range and the detailed practicality of his schemes may be studied in his pamphlets, from those which describe the ideal "gothic" form of government to those which recommend the licensing of beggars or the correction of the English language. In the *Travels*, as elsewhere, his advice is expressed sometimes directly, sometimes by inversion. In the sixth chapter of the first voyage, and generally in his description of the Brobdingnagians, he points to practical devices, such as the public reward of virtue among the Lilliputians, which Europe might well adopt. But he is equally clear, and perhaps more effective, when he suggests the way of life he believes in by a satiric attack upon its opposite. Only a dull intellect could fail to understand that a man who rails at filth advocates cleanliness. The Houyhnhnms and the yahoos represent the extremes between which human behavior may range. Swift certainly did not expect humanity to achieve the height or sink to the depth: he did feel that for the moment, at least, man's tendency was downward, and that strenuous efforts were needed if the trend was to be reversed. To this end he bent his efforts with increasing fervor. Occasionally, as at the conclusion of the *Letter to Sympson*, his missionary zeal expressed itself in a jeremiad:

> I must freely confess, that since my last Return, some Corruptions of my *Yahoo* Nature have revived in me by conversing with a few of your Species, and particularly those of mine own Family, by an unavoidable Necessity; else I should never have attempted so absurd a Project as that of reforming the *Yahoo* Race in this Kingdom; but I have now done with all such visionary Schemes for ever. (Par. 9.)

But some years later, in the *Verses on the Death of Dr. Swift*, he made his defender say of him,

> His Satyr points at no Defect
> But what all Mortals may correct ; . . .[41]

What drove Swift to his occasional outbursts of fury was the consciousness of his own helplessness. In his youth his discontent had been due largely to the postponement of his entry into the world of affairs in a position suited to his capacity. During the few short years of the Oxford-Bolingbroke administration he had employed all his energies in attempts to put into effect certain ideas with which he felt his powerful friends were in sympathy. Then had followed the blasting of his hopes by the triumph of the Whigs, and the gradually growing, bitter conviction that never again in his lifetime would he be in a position of political power. It is hardly to be wondered at that he sometimes allowed himself the relief of savage invective.

It is this savage invective that is responsible for the common belief that Swift was a misanthrope. Swift himself lent some color to this legend by his own statement in a letter already quoted.

> . . . the chief end I propose to myself in all my labours is to vex the world rather than divert it ; and if I could compass that design, without hurting my own person or fortune, I would be the most indefatigable writer you have ever seen, without reading. . . . when you [Pope] think of the world, give it one lash the more at my request. I have ever hated all nations, professions, and communities, and all my love is toward individuals : for instance, I hate the tribe of lawyers, but I love Counsellor Such-a-one, and Judge Such-a-one : so with physicians—I will not speak of my own trade—soldiers, English, Scotch, French, and the rest. But principally I hate and detest that animal called man, although I heartily love John, Peter, Thomas, and so forth. This is the system upon which I have governed myself many years, but do not tell, and so I shall go on till I have done with them. I have got materials toward a treatise, proving the falsity of that definition *animal rationale*, and to show it would be only *rationis capax*. Upon this great foundation of misanthropy, though not in Timon's manner, the whole building of my Travels is erected ; and I never will have peace of mind till all honest men are of my opinion.[42]

The words of this letter themselves show that Swift's "misanthropy" was something far different from the state of mind usually associated with the term. The actions of men in the mass infuriated Swift by their folly and criminality: for individuals he had boundless affection. If his letter had not thus made clear his real attitude toward mankind his whole biography would have done so. It is impossible to ignore the extent of Swift's practical charities, often contrived at the cost of great personal sacrifice of time and money: the daily round of Dublin beggars, the bequest to the hospital for the insane. It is impossible to forget the interest he displayed in the welfare of those who had been placed in his personal care, either as servants or as parishioners: the daily prayers conducted for his domestic staff so quietly that visitors in the house were often unaware of them; the services in the church, day after day and year after year, however thinly attended, lest a worshiper be turned away unministered to. And above all it is impossible to shut one's eyes to Swift's need for human companionship and sympathy. This need Swift often tried to conceal, perhaps because of pride in a cherished self-sufficiency, but his constant seeking out of friends and his correspondence with those who were beyond his reach betray him. Conscience compelled him, as a self-appointed father to the world, to chasten his children, but he wanted their love as well as their obedience. And sometimes this craving for understanding and affection found expression—never more clearly than in the *Verses on the Death of Dr. Swift*, written some five years after *Gulliver's Travels* had fixed in the minds of many contemporaries the fiction of Swift, the enemy of mankind. It is an appeal that from a lesser man would have been pathetic: coming from a genius of the magnitude of Swift it lays bare a tragedy.

Notes

In the notes the following abbreviations of titles are used:

Correspondence. *The Correspondence of Jonathan Swift, D.D.*, ed. F. Elrington Ball (6 vols.), London, 1910.

The Letters of Swift to Ford. *The Letters of Jonathan Swift to Charles Ford*, ed. David Nichol Smith, Oxford, 1935.

Hubbard, *Contributions.* Hubbard, Lucius L., *Contributions towards a Bibliography of Gulliver's Travels*, Chicago, 1922.

Gulliver's Travels (ed. Davis). *Gulliver's Travels*, vol. 11 of *The Prose Writings of Jonathan Swift*, ed. Herbert Davis, Oxford, 1941. (With an introduction by Harold Williams.)

Gulliver's Travels (ed. Dennis). *Gulliver's Travels*, ed. G. Ravenscroft Dennis, vol. 8 of *The Prose Works of Jonathan Swift, D.D.*, ed. Temple Scott, London, 1899.

Gulliver's Travels (ed. Williams). *Gulliver's Travels*, ed. Harold Williams, London, 1926.

References to the text of *Gulliver's Travels* are to book, chapter, and paragraph.

The Text of *Gulliver's Travels*

1 *Correspondence*, 3.364. Ball altered the date of this letter to November 26, relying on a statement in a letter from Arbuthnot to Swift on November 8 (*Correspondence*, 3.357) to the effect that he, Gay and Pope would "meet at Lord Bolingbroke's on Thursday [November 10], in town, at dinner." This does not necessarily mean, as Ball apparently thought, that Pope had not yet come to town: presumably Pope came in from Twickenham only a day or so after the publication of Gulliver.

2 *Correspondence*, 3.276.

3 *Correspondence*, 3.303, note 2, and *passim* thereafter for places from which Swift dates his letters.

4 *The Letters of Swift to Ford*, pp. xx, xxi.

5 See Arbuthnot to Swift, November 8, 1726 (*Correspondence*, 3.357), and Gay and Pope to Swift, November 17, 1726 (*Correspondence*, 3.359).

6 *Correspondence*, 3.328, note 2.

7 Quintana, Ricardo, *The Mind and Art of Jonathan Swift*, London, 1936, p. 295.

8 *Drapier's Letters*, ed. Herbert Davis, Oxford, 1935, pp. lxviii-lxix.

9 *Correspondence*, 3.328, corrected by Gold, Maxwell B., *Swift's Marriage to Stella*, Cambridge, Mass., 1937, p. 178.

10 *Correspondence*, 3.330-331, corrected by Gold, *Swift's Marriage to Stella*, pp. 178-9.

11 *Correspondence*, 3.331.

12 See *Gulliver's Travels* (ed. Williams), p. xxiv; *The Letters of Swift to Ford*, p. xxi; Quintana, *The Mind and Art of Jonathan Swift*, pp. 294-5; *Gulliver's Travels* (ed. Davis), p. xxi.

13 Swift to the Rev. John Worrall, August 13, 1726, *Correspondence*, 3.331-2.

14 *Correspondence*, 3.341.

15 *Correspondence*, 5.180.

16 *Gulliver's Travels* (ed. Dennis), p. xii.

17 References to the text of *Gulliver's Travels* are to book, chapter, and paragraph.

18 *The Letters of Swift to Ford*, p. 154.

19 The original leaf read: "Sometimes our neighbors *want* the things which we *have*, or *have* the things which we *want*; and we both fight, till they take ours and give us theirs." "And," four words from the end of the sentence, was corrected to "or." The phrase "frequent Cause" is altered to "sufficient Cause," the catchword of the verso of the leaf being changed from "frequent" to "sufficient": the first word of the following page, uncanceled, is still "frequent." The change was made to avoid a repetition of "frequent," which appeared a few lines above.

20 *Correspondence*, 3.373.

21 The list is reprinted in Hubbard, *Contributions*, pp. 96-107, and in *Gulliver's Travels* (ed. Williams), pp. 423-31.

22 E.g., by Hubbard, *Contributions*, pp. 45, 52, 53, 95, etc.; by Williams, *Gulliver's Travels*, p. xlvii.

23 *The Letters of Swift to Ford*, p. 156.

24 For the dates and descriptions of the early editions see Hubbard, *Contributions*, p. 127 ff., and *Gulliver's Travels* (ed. Williams), p. lxxxv ff.

25 No one, apparently, takes seriously Faulkner's statement in 1759 that Swift had given him the original manuscript of Gulliver. See *Gulliver's Travels* (ed. Williams), p. xlv, note 2.

26 *Correspondence*, 3.358.

27 Hubbard, *Contributions*, pp. 15-43; *Gulliver's Travels* (ed. Williams), pp. lvi-lxxviii.

28 *Correspondence*, 4.317.

29 *Correspondence*, 4.367.

30 *Correspondence*, 4.431.

31 *Correspondence*, 4.389.

32 *Correspondence*, 4.444.

33 *The Letters of Swift to Ford*, pp. 153-5.

34 *The Letters of Swift to Ford*, p. 156.

35 *The Letters of Swift to Ford*, pp. 161-2.

36 *Correspondence*, 5.1.

37 *Correspondence*, 5.85.

38 *Works* (Faulkner ed., 1735), vol. 1, leaf a4.

39 *Correspondence*, 5.145.

40 *Correspondence*, 5.179.

41 *Correspondence*, 5.224.

42 *Correspondence,* 5.257.

43 *Correspondence,* 5.338.

44 Orrery, John Boyle, 5th Earl of, *Remarks on the Life and Writings of Dr. Jonathan Swift,* London, 1752, pp. 79-81.

45 Orrery, *Remarks,* p. 80.

46 Williams, Harold, Introduction to *Gulliver's Travels* (ed. Davis), p. xxvii. No copy of the *Journal* is available to the author.

47 Hubbard, *Contributions,* p. 61; *Gulliver's Travels* (ed. Williams), p. xlv, and note. No copy of this edition is available to the author.

48 Faulkner was born about 1702 and died on August 28, 1775; see Nichols, John, *Literary Anecdotes,* London, 1812, 3.208-9.

49 For the dates of birth and death in this paragraph see the *Dictionary of National Biography* under the appropriate headings.

50 *Supra,* p. 12.

51 *Works,* vol. 3, leaf following title page.

52 One of these is in the Pierpont Morgan Library, New York; another (which I have not seen) is in the Armagh Public Library. In addition there are annotated copies of the second volume only in the Chapin Library, Williams College, and in the library of Mr. Carroll Wilson, New York.

53 Hubbard, *Contributions,* p. 76; *Gulliver's Travels* (ed. Williams), pp. xlii, xliii, and note 2, p. xliii.

54 *Correspondence,* 3.384.

55 Mr. Harold Williams, in the *Times Literary Supplement* for January 10, 1929 (28.28), has brought forward another argument in favor of his belief that the *Letter to Sympson* was written in the 1730's. In volume 530, pp. 204-6, of miscellaneous Swift manuscripts in the Victoria and Albert Museum, London, he has found a document containing a sentence from the *Letter* and also various scraps of Anglo-Latin of the kind with which Swift amused himself and his Irish friends. Mr. Williams argues that since Swift indulged in this amusement most frequently in the 1730's, and since the sentence from the *Letter* appears to be a trial draft contemporaneous with the Anglo-Latin, the document strengthens his case. But there exist *jeux d'esprit* of this kind by Swift as early as 1723 (see *Correspondence,* 3.177), and until the particular Anglo-Latin sentences are more accurately dated it is difficult to estimate the value of this evidence.

56 1728 is, of course, the cube of twelve: see *Gulliver's Travels,* 1.3.20.

57 Hubbard, *Contributions,* p. 57.

58 Dunlop, O[live] Jocelyn, *English Apprenticeship and Child Labour,* London, 1912, pp. 166, 167; 258, 259.

59 Dunlop, *English Apprenticeship,* pp. 98, 99.

60 Copies of *The Mariner's Magazine* are not readily accessible. The passage which Swift borrowed is quoted at length in *Gulliver's Travels* (ed. Williams), pp. 469-70, from the third edition of Sturmy's book (1684), pp. 15-16. The reading here is (correctly) "tacks," as it is in all editions I have been able to consult.

61 Hubbard, *Contributions,* p. 124.

62 Hubbard, *Contributions,* p. 63.

63 Hubbard, *Contributions,* p. 66.

64 Hubbard, *Contributions,* p. 67.

65 Hubbard, *Contributions,* p. 68.

66 Hubbard, *Contributions*, p. 71.

67 In a letter from Swift to Ford, written on October 9, 1733, Swift, in requesting the use of Ford's interleaved copy of the *Travels*, said, ". . . it will be extreme difficult for me to correct [Gulliver] by any other means, with so ill a memory, and in so bad a State of health." (*Letters to Ford*, p. 155.) And in another letter to Ford, dated November 20, 1733, Swift forgets he wrote five pamphlets which he composed during Queen Anne's reign, among them *A New Journey to Paris*. Nichol Smith, in a note (p. 163) calls this "A notable lapse of memory."

The Geography and Chronology of *Gulliver's Travels*

1 Craik, Sir Henry, *Selections from Swift*, London, 1893, pp. 441-4.

2 *Gulliver's Travels* (ed. Dennis), in the notes, *passim*.

3 *Gulliver's Travels* (ed. Williams), pp. lxxix, lxxx.

4 *Gulliver's Travels* (ed. Williams), pp. 459-90 *passim*.

5 "The Geography of *Gulliver's Travels*," *J.E.G.P.*, 40.214 (1941).

6 See Williams, Harold, *Dean Swift's Library*, Cambridge, 1932.

7 *Correspondence*, 3. 134, 137; *The Letters of Swift to Ford*, pp. 36-7.

8 This map, which is included in various atlases, was apparently the most recent Moll map of the world at the time when Swift began the composition of the *Travels*, though an examination of other Moll maps between 1709 and 1745 indicates that the cartographer made no changes in his data during this period which would have affected Gulliver's geography.

Frederick Bracher has recently published (*Huntington Library Quarterly*, 8.1.59 [1944]) an article entitled "The Maps in *Gulliver's Travels*," in which he shows that the artist who drew the maps in the first edition used Moll's map of 1719. He agrees with the present author that neither Swift nor any of his friends was in any way responsible for the 1726 maps with their numerous errors, and gives reasons for believing that they were drawn by John Sturt and engraved by Robert Sheppard.

9 The map of the Gulliverian hemisphere in this volume is based on Moll's map of the world.

10 Moore, John R., "The Geography of *Gulliver's Travels*," *J.E.G.P.*, 40.217-20 (1941).

11 *Gulliver's Travels* (ed. Dennis), p. 295, note.

12 The late Professor Walter Graham pointed out to me that eight months (as indicated in the first edition) was the normal time for a voyage from England to India, according to the eighteenth-century records of the East India Company.

Personal and Political Satire in *Gulliver's Travels*

1 *Correspondence*, 3.359-60.

2 *Gulliver's Travels*, ed. W. Cooke Taylor, London, [1840], p. 52, note.

3 Firth, Sir Charles, "The Political Significance of *Gulliver's Travels*," *Proceedings of the British Academy*, 9.237-39, 242-3 (1919-20) : reprinted in Firth, Sir Charles, *Essays, Historical and Literary*, Oxford, 1938, pp. 210-11, 217-19.

4 *The Poems of Jonathan Swift*, ed. Harold Williams, Oxford, 1937, 1.141-5.

5 Stanhope, Philip Henry, Earl, *The Reign of Queen Anne until the Peace of Utrecht*, London, 1908, 2.237.

6 Firth, Sir Charles, *op. cit.* (1919-20), pp. 242-3; (1938), pp. 217-19; on p. 218 (1938), he notes that Nottingham had been First Lord of the Admiralty from 1680 to 1684, and thereafter prided himself on his knowledge of naval affairs.

7 *Correspondence*, 2.199.

8 MacKnight, Thomas, *The Life of Henry St. John, Viscount Bolingbroke*, London, 1863, pp. 438-40.

9 As examples note the following excerpts from the charges against Bolingbroke, as reported in *The Historical Register*, vol. 2, 1724:

I. He the said Henry Viscount Bolingbroke, then being one of her Majesty's principal Secretaries of State, and of her most honourable Privy Council, but having enter'd into a most treacherous confederacy with the ministers and emissaries of France, to frustrate the just hopes and expectations of her Majesty and her people, by disuniting the confederacy, at the most critical juncture, when they were ready to reap the fruits of so many triumphs over the common enemy, and most wickedly intending, so far as in him lay, to enable the French King, so exhausted and vanquished as he had been, on all occasions, to carry his designs by a peace glorious to him, and to the ruin of the victorious Allies, . . . did . . . maliciously and wickedly form a most treacherous and pernicious contrivance and confederacy with other evil-disposed persons, then also of her Majesty's Privy Council, to set on foot a private, separate, dishonourable, and destructive negociation of peace, between Great Britain and France. . . . (pp. 2, 3.)

II. That the French King, . . . having, with the privity, and by the contrivance of the said Viscount Bolingbroke, and others, sent over Mons. Mesnager into England, to carry on a separate and clandestine negociation of peace, he, the said Viscount Bolingbroke, did afterwards . . . secretly, and unlawfully, and without any colour of authority, meet, confer, and treat with the said Sieur Mesnager, on the negociations of peace between Great Britain and France. . . . (p. 4.)

And the said Henry Viscount Bolingbroke did afterwards, in violation of his oath and high trust, falsely and treacherously advise her late Majesty to sign powers to several persons for concluding, on her behalf, a pernicious and destructive convention on the said subject of peace with France; And on or about the . . . 27th of September, 1711, a dishonourable, destructive, and fatal treaty or convention, was concluded, and sign'd by the said Sieur Mesnager, on the part of France, and by the Earl of Dartmouth, and the said Viscount, being then two of her Majesty's Principal Secretaries of State, and of her Privy Council, on the part of her Majesty, by virtue only of a warrant under her Majesty's sign-manual, under the Signet, directed to themselves, but not countersign'd, and without the least knowledge or participation of the Allies; in which treaty the immediate interests of Great Britain were given up to France, and the Duke of Anjou being therein admitted to remain King of Spain, the balance of power, and the liberties of Europe, were thrown into the hands of the House of Bourbon. (pp. 4, 5.)

See also *The Tryal of Robert Earl of Oxford*, London, 1717, pp. 6-27, especially Article V with reference to Nottingham's restrictions on the terms of peace.

10 See *A Report from the Committee . . . of the House of Commons to Examine Christopher Layer and Others*, 1722 (1723), pp. 37-52.

11 *The Poems of Jonathan Swift* (ed. Williams), 2.550.

12 *Gulliver's Travels* (ed. G. A. Aitken, Temple Classics), London, 1896, pp. 399-401.

13 *Gulliver's Travels* (ed. Dennis), pp. 178-9.

14 Firth, Sir Charles, *op. cit.* (1938), p. 239.

15 *Gulliver's Travels* (ed. Dennis), p. 181, note.

16 Firth, Sir Charles, *op. cit.* (1938), p. 230.

17 Melville, Lewis, *The South Sea Bubble*, London, 1921, pp. 75-110.

18 *Gulliver's Travels* (ed. Taylor), p. 314, note 1.

19 Beeching, H. C., *Francis Atterbury*, London, 1909, chapter X. See also note 10 above.

20 Bolingbroke to Ford, Jan. 1, 1722 (N.S.): "if you write to your humble servant La Tour, you may please to direct to him chez Messieurs de Moracin et la Borde Rue Berthin poirée a Paris." *The Letters of Swift to Ford*, p. 236.

21 Ballard, Colin, *The Great Earl of Peterborough*, London, 1929, pp. 213, 241.

22 *Ibid.*, p. 229.

23 *The Prose Works of Jonathan Swift*, ed. Temple Scott, London, 1911, 5.77-8.

24 *Journal to Stella*, ed. J. K. Moorhead (Everyman's Library), London, n.d., p. 438.

25 The Earl of Oxford.

26 Gold, Maxwell, *Swift's Marriage to Stella*, pp. 176-7.

The Significance of *Gulliver's Travels*

1 Orrery, John Boyle, 5th Earl of, *Remarks on the Life and Writings of Dr. Jonathan Swift*, London, 1752, pp. 195-6.

2 Swift, Deane, *An Essay upon the Life . . . of Dr. Jonathan Swift*, London, 1755, p. 182.

3 Delany, Patrick, *Observations upon Lord Orrery's Remarks*, London, 1754, p. 100.

4 *The Letters of Swift to Ford*, p. 92.

5 *Correspondence*, 3.113.

6 *Correspondence*, 3.133.

7 *Correspondence*, 3.134.

8 *The Letters of Swift to Ford*, pp. 96, 97.

9 *The Letters of Swift to Ford*, p. 238.

10 *The Letters of Swift to Ford*, pp. 100, 101.

11 *The Letters of Swift to Ford*, pp. 102, 103.

12 *The Letters of Swift to Ford*, p. 108.

13 *Correspondence*, 3.210.

14 *Correspondence*, 3.259.

15 *The Letters of Swift to Ford*, p. 122.

16 *The Letters of Swift to Ford*, p. 125.

17 *Correspondence*, 3.267.

18 *Correspondence*, 3.269.

19 *Correspondence*, 3.276-8.

20 *Correspondence*, 3.284.

21 *Correspondence*, 3.293.

22 *Correspondence*, 3.296-7.

23 For a more detailed statement of this theory see Quintana, Ricardo, *The Mind and Art of Jonathan Swift*, pp. 289-94.

24 Spence, Joseph, *Anecdotes, Observations and Characters* (ed. S. W. Singer), London, 1820, p. 10.

25 *Correspondence*, 2.162-3.

26 *Correspondence*, 2.288.

27 *Correspondence*, 3.359.

28 *The Works of Alexander Pope*, London, 1741, 2.242. The *Essay Concerning the Origine of Sciences* had previously been published (inaccurately) in *Miscellanies. The Third Volume*, London, 1732, pp. 98 ff.

29 Spence, Joseph, *Anecdotes*, p. 201.

30 *The Works of Alexander Pope*, London, 1741, 2.65.

31 Swift's letter of October 15, 1720 (*Correspondence*, 3.68) refers to the South Sea Bubble, and just two months later he writes to Ford (*The Letters of Swift to Ford*, p. 88) to arrange for the publication in London of the verses on the South Sea Bubble, which, as the letter shows, he had promised to send Ford, presumably before the latter's departure from Ireland about the middle of November.

32 *The Letters of Swift to Ford*, p. 92.

33 *Correspondence*, 3.113.

34 *Supra*, p. 97.

35 This is on the assumption that Swift began the *Travels* between January and April, 1721 (*vide supra*, pp. 97 and 106-7), and finished the first two voyages about June or July, 1722 (*vide supra*, p. 98).

36 The fourth voyage was finished by January, 1723-4: see the letter to Ford, *supra*, p. 99.

37 See the letter to Ford, *supra*, p. 99.

38 The draft was apparently finished by August, 1725: see the letter to Ford, *supra*, p. 100.

39 This assumes that Swift did not finish the emendations until shortly before he went to England in the spring of 1726. It is, of course, possible to interpret Swift's statements in his letter to Pope on September 29, 1725 (*supra*, pp. 100-101) to mean that the emendations had been completed by that time.

40 *Correspondence*, 3.407. In the original French the passage runs: "Si donc les livres du sieur Gulliver ne sont calcules que pour les isles Britanniques, ce voyageur doit passer pour un tres pitoyable ecrivain. Les memes vices et les memes folies regnent partout; du moins, dans tous les pays civilisés de l'Europe: et l'auteur, que n'ecrit que pour une ville, une province, un royaume, ou meme un siecle, merite si peu d'être traduit, qu'il ne merite pas d'etre lû."

41 *The Poems of Jonathan Swift* (ed. Harold Williams), 2.571 (ll. 463-4).

42 *Correspondence*, 3.276-7.